Letters
from Eden

10/24/93
A moments
impression of an
ad Cooper's (eye
yolk-orange) who
made a sweep
of the orchard &
yard, then settled
in Hendersnett's oak,
tucked up a foot,
preened, and was
off again.
very pale peach
front

An imm. golden eagle over the
tower - #174 for ar preserve
March 29, 2000 *[signature]*

LETTERS FROM EDEN

A Year at Home, in the Woods

Julie Zickefoose

HOUGHTON MIFFLIN COMPANY

BOSTON   NEW YORK

2006

For information about permission to reproduce selections from this book, write to Permissions, Houghton Mifflin Company, 215 Park Avenue, New York, New York 10003.

Visit our Web site: www.houghtonmifflinbooks.com.

Library of Congress Cataloging-in-Publication Data
Zickefoose, Julie.
    Letters from Eden : a year at home, in the woods/Julie Zickefoose.
    p. cm.
ISBN-13: 978-0-618-57308-0
ISBN-10: 0-618-57308-9
1. Bird watching — Ohio 2. Natural history — Ohio.
3. Zickefoose, Julie — Homes and haunts — Ohio. I. Title.
    QL684.O3Z53 2006
    508.771 — dc22   2006000477

Book design by Anne Chalmers, in memory of Diana Weber Palms
Typefaces: Aries, Monotype Centaur

Excerpt from "Gift" reprinted by permission of Louisiana State University Press from *Autumn Grasses: Poems by Margaret Gibson*. Copyright © 2003 by Margaret Gibson.

Printed in the United States of America

DOC 10 9 8 7 6 5 4 3 2 1

For Bill: my light, life, and love.

For Mom: strong, selfless, and wise.

For Dad: restless, curious, earthy.

And for Jeanne, who teaches with grace.

Acknowledgments

I AM THINKING BACK over the past decade, playing a chicken-and-egg game. There would be no *Letters from Eden* without my husband, Bill Thompson III, who asked me to write a column called "Watcher at the Window." Bill and I wouldn't be together if he hadn't called me up in 1991 to ask me to paint a cover for *Bird Watcher's Digest*. Neither Bill nor the magazine would be on the planet without his parents, publishers Bill Jr. and Elsa Thompson. Bill's brother Andy, now publisher, continues to support my work. Managing editor Debbie Griffith is a quiet delight to work with. I am deeply grateful to these brave people, the Thompson family, and the magazine they created out of love, their children's college fund, and thin air. *Bird Watcher's Digest* accepted the first piece I ever submitted for publication, anywhere, and twenty years, seventeen cover paintings, and almost a hundred articles and columns later, *BWD* remains my first and last resort as a writer and illustrator. Through it, I've been given an audience, and the chance to show them things I find lovely and interesting. And it's given me Bill, Phoebe, and Liam, my heartbeats, and the home we've made together in the Appalachian foothills. Thank you for dragging me away from the coast, love. You were right. We've made our own weather.

My best friend and creative soulmate Shila Wilson swoops in and saves me on a daily basis. More than anyone, she's made this East Coast refugee feel at home in southeast Ohio.

Straight out of college I worked for The Nature Conservancy's Connecticut chapter. Dr. and Mrs. Richard Goodwin allowed me to live and wonder in a small cottage on the Burnham Brook Preserve. Thank you, Dick and Esther, for the rent-free decade of woods time. I'm forever indebted to Rob Braunfield for his love and aesthetic guidance. The Artist's Group: Jim Coe, Mike DiGiorgio, Cindy House, John Baumlin, Larry Barth, Brenda Carter, Barry Van Dusen, Debby Kaspari, and David Quinn, make me feel part of a modern movement, or at the very least, a wildly creative, loving family. A new chapter in my writing opened in 2004 when afternoon anchor Melissa Block suggested that I submit commentaries to National Public Radio's *All Things Considered.* Editor Ellen Silva cheers, steers, polishes, and always asks for more. She keeps me on the air month after month and scribbling happily in my notebook as I wind down the country roads. I'm deeply grateful for the voice and audience NPR has given me.

In the beginning, I painted and drew for other people's articles, but as I spent more and more time in the woods, there were stories I had to tell. Over time, I realized I was happiest when I was decorating my own writing. *Letters from Eden* is an unusual book, with its nearly equal emphasis on text and art, and as such it's a bit of an experiment. I thank Russ Galen, Houghton Mifflin, and my editor Lisa White for believing that this alchemy would make something beautiful. Production editor Shelley Berg and jacket designer Martha Kennedy shaped this collection into a book, and designer Anne Chalmers has made each page a joy to look at. You've bettered my wildest dreams.

Last, I thank my parents, Ida and Dale. Ida encouraged us, her five kids, to do our absolute best, without ever letting on that she thought we were anything special. (Bob, Barbara, Nancy, and Micky, you are something special indeed.) I'm still trying to figure out how Mom did that, so I can do it for my kids. And Dad, you showed me everything. Listening to your stories I learned how to tell them, too. Thank you.

Contents

Five box turtles, all life-size, hatched starting Day 108
(10/04/90) from a nest laid 6/18. It took 'til the
morning of 10/09 for all five to dig the 2½" to
the surface. The female made her nest only inches
from the edge of Dolbia Hill Road in East Haddam, CT.
I protected it and another box turtle nest with
weighted cages, foiling attempts by a raccoon on
one and a black rat snake on this one (on hatching night).
The pink yolk sac pulses as the turtle breathes. It had
shrunk flush with the plastron by 5 days of age. The
hatchlings gained strength each day and proved impossible
to hold in one hand by the second day. Released 10/10/90.

Zickefoose 10/9-10/90 direct from life

Foreword

JUST WHEN we're about to fledge — in high school or in college — the rumors start. Rumors about the "real world." It is somewhere "out there," and, we are told, we had better get ready for it.

And just what is this "real world"? To survey all too much of modern America, it would seem to be a world of concrete, steel, asphalt, cars, malls, and chemical-drenched lawns. (Sometimes relieved by the occasional vacation trip — usually to someplace where you can still glimpse some piece of the natural world, a mountain or forest or ocean, at least from a hotel window.) The real world, we're led to believe, is the modern world, the urban world, the "built" world — built by money. Our success in it is measured by the size of the paycheck, the house, the car, and the sort of security that money can buy.

What a crock.

This book is about the *real* world: the lush, green, breathing, loving, feverish, hungry, joyous, *living* world. It's made of soil and scent, birdsongs and frog croaks, eggs cradled in down-lined nests and carcasses split by talons. It's a world composed of moonlight, raindrops, the sweet spring scent of maple blossoms, turkey tracks in winter snow. It's a world where progress is measured in the sputtering first flights of baby wrens, the accrued knowledge of daily walks among the same woodland path, or a child's wonder as a tree swallow swoops to accept nesting material from her hand. It's the world captured in Julie Zickefoose's luminous paintings and eloquent words.

This is the world we were literally made for — a world in which humans are just one of many species whose daily dramas we follow with intense and consuming interest. Think of it: For all but the last few moments of our existence as a species, evolutionarily speaking, humans have been hunter-gatherers. We depended upon the natural world — the *real* world — for everything: food, shelter, clothing, medicine, even art, worship, and inspiration. The natural world is where our kind perfected "the wholeness of all we think of as culture," wrote Paul Shepherd, the scholar of human ecology. No wonder our interest is acute.

Because I sometimes write books for children, I am often asked where children get their fascination with animals and plants. I answer it's the nature of our species, encoded in our genes. For hundreds of thousands of years, if a person didn't pay attention to the plants and animals and weather, she couldn't find anything to eat, was overtaken by storms, or something came and ate her while she wasn't looking. The misfit genes of those who didn't care for the natural world were pruned by the appetites of hungry smilodons. No wonder observing the natural world provides us with deep, abiding joy. It is the key to life itself.

These days, of course, few hunter-gatherer societies survive. In America, child advocates like Richard Louv tell us with growing alarm that our children can more readily identify a Pokemon character than an oak tree. But even in our most urban pursuits, our genetic heritage shows: Why do men love to chase a little ball around a big field, or watch others doing so? What could be more like hunters chasing a small animal — an animal, incidentally, that we call game? And why do women love to shop? We are shopper-gatherers now, even though we've forgotten where all the berries are. No wonder the mall provides only shallow satisfaction. No wonder our children are growing up on Prozac. We are in danger of forgetting how to live.

It's not that we don't know something is wrong. Never has there been such a proliferation of self-help books, seminars, and twelve-step programs promising to help us feel less lost and miserable on the planet we used to call home. In our new, artificial world, apart from nature, we still hunger for the real world — the home that made us human. We are always looking for Eden.

And that is why this book is important.

Letters from Eden brings us eight years' worth of stories and seasons "at home in the woods." It is written and illustrated by a woman with an exceptionally keen eye and large heart. Julie is a nature writer and artist with impressive credentials: She has contributed more than forty articles and seventeen cover paintings to *Bird Watcher's Digest*. She has painted color posters and illustrated educational materials for the U.S. Fish and Wildlife Service, the American Ornithologists' Union, the Academy of Natural Sciences, and the Cornell Lab of Ornithology. She lectures all over the country; her writing enlivens books, magazine articles, and National Public Radio. But what makes this book such a joy comes from talents you won't find listed on her CV.

One of Julie's greatest accomplishments is that, with her birder-editor husband, Bill Thompson III, she was able to not just find but create her own Eden. "Heaven," wrote Thoreau, "is under our feet as well as over our heads," and Julie and Bill found theirs on eighty acres of overgrown pasture in the Appalachian woodlands of southeast Ohio. Rather than bulldoze the place and build a McMansion, with careful stewardship they have turned it into a nature sanctuary — and the perfect spot from which to observe those creatures she loves best: bullfrogs and indigo buntings, butterflies and vultures, sugarsnap peas and sunflowers, her blue-eyed son and his red-haired older sister.

Julie is a woman of extraordinary generosity. She asks her hairdresser for the clippings that fall beneath her chair after each haircut so she can give them to the birds for nesting material. When she found her daughter had run over a copperhead's tail with her bike, she gently captured the snake and released the venomous animal elsewhere, so both species could be safe from each other. But then again, what would you expect from a woman who as a student at Harvard rescued a chicken from the cruelties of lab experimentation and raised it in her dorm room? It all makes for stories that are unexpected, touching, and hilarious — sometimes all at once.

But perhaps Julie's greatest talent is for paying attention — doing what we were made for. Most of the stories captured in these paintings, drawings, and prose are probably similar to those happening in your own backyard — even if you live in a suburb or city. Julie knows where to find and how to see the dramas that unfold all around us — right here in the *real* world, the natural world that was our first and, still, our proper home.

Julie is, by her own admission, a woman "moved to rapture by half a possum and two owl droppings." In other words, she is a woman who knows how to live.

Here is her manual of how to do it. Welcome home.

—SY MONTGOMERY

Preface

LATELY I've been reading stories of nature study in far-flung and dangerous places, stories written by women of courage. To comb through my own writings, ruminations on the natural world just outside my door, has been a humbling counterpoint to their adventures. Granted, it's a pretty nice yard: eighty acres of Appalachian woodland surrounded by a patchwork of forest and agricultural land. I watch my neighbors: coyotes, copperheads, gnatcatchers, and bluebirds. I walk through their woods, and I'm lucky enough to come to know some of them.

There is nothing really extraordinary going on in this bit of forest. The creatures who live here go about their affairs much as they do anywhere else. Box turtles roam a seasonal route, showing up at the same place year after year at the same time. Bullfrogs leap from the water to snap up birds. Bluebirds and Carolina wrens sometimes have threesomes. These things are extraordinary only if we know they happen. My work is to notice them.

These essays were written over a span of eight years. Our two children were born in that time, and you'll find them toddling through the pages—speaking complete sentences here, still nursing a few pages later. Seasonal change was the strongest organizational element I could find for this collection, and I thought it would be harmonious to travel through a year from winter to spring, through summer and fall, back to winter. I hope my incredible shrinking children aren't too much of a distraction. They're part of the story, too. They keep me here at home, briefly slipping the sweet bonds of motherhood to watch, walk, and think. Without them, I might not have looked so closely at this bit of woods, or appreciated it so much.

My alarm clock — he sings every morning under the bedroom window

WINTER

January Thaw

AT LAST! One of those blazing blue winter days that seem to grace New England all the time but are much too rare here in the cloud-shrouded Mid-Ohio Valley. It was still frigid at daybreak when I looked out to see a bluebird emerge from its roosting place: a PVC pipe elbow tucked onto a shelf under our garage eave. As I watched, another four bluebirds popped out of our martin gourd cluster. After nine years, we're still waiting for martins, but the gourds make splendid roost boxes in the meantime.

Instead of lining out as they usually do for the fallow fields on the road, the bluebirds began to sing, scold, and chatter. They broke up into pairs, and each claimed a nest box. Waving their wings, the males fluttered above while the females poked their heads in the entrance holes. The winter games had begun! It's little wonder that we love bluebirds so, when they are such easy optimists about spring's return. The house finches and Carolina wrens have barely begun to warble in late January when bluebirds open up to full voice. Like us, they know that the snow and ice will return many times before nesting season truly begins. But they seem to love to play at territorial battles and courtship games, helpless to resist the lengthening days and increasing warmth of the sun. Standing with the door open, listening to their caroling, I decided it would be a good day to wash and finally hang out the bedding. In our own ways, we're all playing house on this brink-of-spring day.

I've been walking nearly every day this January, walking off cabin fever on a two-mile hike through the woods and overgrown meadows near our house. The relief is steep, and there are places where I have to take off my gloves and hat to dump a little heat as I climb. Right after New Year's, I took a hand clipper to the multiflora rose, smilax, and black raspberry brambles that lacerated my legs on the first few pushes through. Now I can gallop along if the wind is raw, or dawdle if the sun is warm.

A lovely thing happens to me on that trail that happens nowhere else. When I start the walk, I'm invariably chewing over the events of the day or week, often grinding my teeth and muttering as I replay some unpleasant exchange. It feels as if my brain has a cramp. Like the steady pressure of a masseuse, the hike works on that knot, and along about the overlook, where I usually see a red-tailed hawk, the mental muscle suddenly relaxes. The things I should have said, the musical brain-worms that were taking up my thoughts, are suddenly silenced, replaced by the trill of kinglets and the crunch of leaves underfoot. Like a coot, I must patter over the surface for a good distance before taking to the air.

Finally released, I'm open to the subtle sounds and sights around me. Even through layers of fleece and nylon, I hear the notes of winter feeding flocks. I try to get good looks at the birds as they pass all around me. I focus my binoculars on a golden-crowned kinglet just a yard off the forest floor. Backed by a curtain of rusty fawn beech leaves, he turns to face me. His gleaming cap of sunny yellow, its orange center stripe, its ebony edging, all knock the air out of me. I wonder, when I see a kinglet like this, whether they might be as the manatee is to the mermaid. Did some Druid storyteller see a goldcrest materialize out of deep forest, hovering by his face, and invent fairies on the spot?

A subadult — only a white fringe under chin gives it away

10/2/97
in a strong SW breeze
He disappeared while I looked down and was hunting a wolf spider when I looked up

I skim along, waiting for the next revelation. Coming down the steep valley I call the Chute, my eye is arrested by a brilliant splash of crimson in the leaf litter. A large opossum, vividly opened, lies in the streambed. It's very fresh and must have been killed just last night. Carefully, I kneel at the crime scene, searching for clues—tracks, stray hairs, feathers—anything that will tell me whodunit. Small puncture wounds cover the animal's face, and his mouth is stuffed with leaves, gathered in his death throes. Otherwise he's intact, not torn up as he would be had he tangled with a coyote. I surmise that he has been surprised from behind and that he has died slowly and rather badly. Finally, I see a freshly cast pellet off to the side, which confirms my growing suspicion that only a great horned owl could have subdued such a large animal.

The fact that the carcass is still here pretty much rules out a coyote as the killer; the big canid would have carried it off to cache. While an owl, given time and the right grip, could have killed this big old possum, it would have been forced to eat its fill on the spot and come back for subsequent meals until the carcass was light enough to airlift out. Satisfied with my sleuthing, I rise and continue the walk, eager to return and get another piece of the puzzle tomorrow.

I hurry down the Chute the next afternoon, looking forward to seeing whether the owl has returned. The possum is gone, cleanly and completely. There are two large splats in its place, yellowish white and puddled. Great horned owl droppings, I'm as sure as if I'd seen the owl itself. Hawks shoot their droppings out, leaving a long white stripe; owls drop them straight down, into puddles. I realize I am laughing and talking to myself, and I have to laugh again at the thought of a woman moved to rapture by half a possum and two owl droppings.

Saturday comes. Though Bill is trying to get packed for a trip, I wheedle until he agrees to come with me on the hike. We talk until the overlook, then fall into comfortable silence, breathing to the rhythm of our tramping boots. It snowed last night, and we get to see the hidden life on our land, finding deer, fox, and coyote prints. We come down into the Chute and put up first one ruffed grouse, then a second. A pileated woodpecker begins to complain, its uneven yelps speeding up as it swoops into a broken beech. Its mate follows. A deer starts up from its bed on the slope to our right and *ka-thunks* off. The pileateds' *kukk*ing rises to a crescendo, and a very large owl suddenly flops into sight, beating hard across the trail, over the streambed where the possum died, and over the next rise. Buffy-fawn below, its wings laced with the same color, it can only be a great horned, the first one we've sighted on our land. Not all of my wildwood sleuthing ties up so nicely.

Time's a-wasting. The sheets, four loads of them, are flapping in the January wind. The sun is warming; there are fairies to be seen and murders to be solved. I'm taking off.

Adaptation

IT'S A CAROLINA WREN–killing winter. Subfreezing temperatures and snow cover for weeks at a time knock their populations, which had burgeoned in the past few mild winters, right back down. They're insectivores, searching out dormant spiders, cocoons, egg cases, and the like. Almost all of them die in winters like this, except those that have learned to exploit humans. I'm keeping our two pairs going with peanut butter suet, which I mix up for them on the stove. It smells so good when I'm stirring it up that I'm tempted to stick a finger into it, but then I remind myself that it's got a pound of lard in it and stop. More lard I don't need.

Winters like this one force birds into doing things they might not ordinarily resort to. Starlings, for instance, are extremely wary birds, but they seem to lose that wariness when the ground is frozen, and they mob feeders in squabbling flocks. They hang upside down from suet cages and hover at tube feeders. They wait hungrily for me to throw out the day's compost, and they pick greedily through our leavings. When a pork roast I'd bought turned into pressed wood in the oven, I put it out for them. By nightfall, they had reduced it to a few clean bones. Piranhas would hang their heads. And darting in between their portly bodies were two Carolina wrens, gobbling down what I'm sure was their first roast pork dinner.

There's not a whole lot to do on such frigid days but work and eat, and therein lies a big (fat) problem. No matter how cold it is, I try to get out every afternoon to walk a loop through the woods and fields around our house. I love walking in fall and winter, and besides, the vegetation is so thick it's impossible to do from June through September. In October, I go out with heavy loppers and hand pruners and fight the briars and sumac back from my rutted path, worn from almost fourteen years of such walking.

Four ruffed grouse and eleven turkeys live along this two-mile loop, and I know where they feed and rest. The grouse take shelter under Japanese honeysuckle bowers, which, when they're snow-covered, make a passable grouse house. Much as I hate to flush them, I love the sight and thunder of their russet bodies and banded, fanned tails barreling through the underbrush. One weekend, while walking the loop with a dear friend who's getting into bird watching, the orchard grouse hopped up onto a limb to get a better look at us. We were starstruck by his jet-black ruffs and neat barring, his stripes and spangles, and the jaunty topknot he raised and lowered as he looked us over.

The next two days, he was there in his honeysuckle bower, and I brought handfuls of cracked corn and suet pellets, sunflower and millet, and tossed them in for him to eat. He never moved a muscle. I left him there, considering this sudden bounty, and walked the loop. An hour later, I returned and was stunned to find, via their trident-shaped tracks, that six wild turkeys had found the bower and its food, run the grouse out, and scratched the living daylights out of his shelter. I didn't know whether to be amused or mad, so decided on a mix. I hadn't done that lovely grouse a favor after all.

I decided to leave the grouse to his honeysuckle berries and rosehips and strew a little shelled corn under the pines in our backyard. The next morning, six turkeys were there pecking about, looking like great black vultures, so unexpected against the snow. The following morning, there were eleven, and eleven have returned each day, eagerly accepting their first-ever subsidized meal plan. They're all beardless immatures but for two big hens on watch all the time. I can see them processing the situation, deciding that we are not to be feared after all. Flushed, they no longer fly but saunter away. They greet my emergence from the house with loud, hollow *PUTT* calls—they're watching from the woods all day long. It's a great pleasure to know that their crops are full of good corn in such brutal weather. And even as I enjoy watching them posture and joust with each other, I wonder what will come of this new feeding program. I imagine those huge strong feet raking through my flower beds. I know of someone in upstate New York who started feeding turkeys, only to have them peck—hard—at their provider's glass

Jan 8 04

Then they stand alert, like this.
They start the frisk standing
alert, too. It goes:
What? What's that? A coyote!
Come to kill us all! Ack! Ack!
Dodge! Run! Oh. Guess not.
Perhaps it's analogous to "dread flights"
in terns, a fire drill q sorts.

There is a sudden cavort, the
wings flapped, a dodge to the
side, a short weaving run —
that they do on their way
to and from the feeding area.
They aren't startled, and don't
run — it looks more like
friskiness. Both hens & toms do it.

patio doors when the corn ran out. Give
'em an inch, as the saying goes . . .

I think about our deep and ever-
growing relationship with the
wildlife on these eighty acres. Our
presence here is more than be-
nign; we actively help the
birds and animals when
times are hard. As I
write, a whitetail
doe and her
button-buck
fawn are moving in,
dark against pale
snow, to clean up spilled
sunflower seed under the
bird feeders and find the few

handfuls of corn I tossed out for them just before dusk. Phoebe is kneeling by the
studio window, watching them. I believe she knows, even at six, how lucky she is
to have such neighbors. From their behavior, it's clear to me that these deer, these
turkeys, bluebirds, wrens, woodpeckers—the countless birds who come to our
yard for food and shelter—recognize us as harmless and willingly take the olive
branch we extend to them. I like knowing that the band of chickadees and titmice
I see on my daily walk may well have my sunflower seeds in their tiny crops, fuel
for the coming night. I like making eye contact with the hairy woodpecker at the
corner of the orchard, knowing that she is the one I see at the peanut feeder in

These twin fawns
ate the same plants
the whole time I
watched. The smaller
still showed spots on either
side of her spine.

the morning. I like following the turkeys' tracks to see what else besides corn they
are finding to eat. I love hearing the ruffed grouse start to drum in March, the
sounds coming from where I know each one lives. Getting out each day to be
among them, then returning home to watch them come to me—that gets me
through the winter. Spring and summer slip by in a joyous, colorful blur, but en-
joying winter takes a little more work—a little more adaptation—from all of us.

Grosbeaks: A Remembrance

IT MUST have been 1967. Our family room was done up in Early American: Bald eagles with spread wings were on everything. Four Audubon prints, a little faded, hung over the couch—the Harris's hawk, the whimbrel, the bobwhite, and the wild turkey hen with brood. I stared at them for hours, especially when I was home sick, lying in luxury, wondering what it would be like to do nothing but draw birds instead of going to school.

That winter was snowy for Richmond, Virginia—big blankets of heavy, wet snow that made a mess of the streets and the southern drivers, not to mention their cars. I loved nothing more than awakening on a school day to see that special snow light peeping under the shade, the white, pure light that sets a child's heart singing with the hope of sleds instead of homework.

On one such morning, I tore downstairs to find my mother and father craning their necks out the kitchen window at a flock of strange birds in our sweet gum tree. They were mustard yellow, black, and white, though some were gray, with pied wings. A ringing *cleer!* call punched the stillness and snow quiet. Several sat on the simple table feeder that my father had welded from a pipe and a steel plate. They had already cleaned up the sunflower seed there and seemed to be looking for more. We'd never seen anything like them. "Giant goldfinches!" I yelled as I

10-30-93
They stayed from
8:15 to 12:15, ranks
swelling from six to 21!

ran for my well-worn
*National Geographic Song and Gar-
den Birds of North America.*

They were evening grosbeaks,
of course, and there were sixty of
them, a flock such as I've never had since
at any feeder. They showed up around
Christmas and stayed into spring. We began
buying striped sunflower seed in fifty-pound bags. This
was a pretty extravagant purchase in 1967. I got up early every morning to put seed
out for the flock, which my father referred to as "Julie's chickens." We loved to
watch them squabble over the food, and we loved the way they looked, hanging in

the trees like big ornaments. At about the same time, my father, who always spent his free time in his basement workshop, became secretive and wouldn't let me watch him work as he always had. I suspected he was making something for me.

On Christmas morning, I awoke to the familiar sound of grosbeaks fighting and feeding, but it was unusually loud. On the dining room windowsill was a feeder, the grandest one ever made, with a long dowel perch and a Plexiglas top to keep the seed dry, with drainage holes and a new coat of gray paint. It was three feet long, and the grosbeaks crammed into it by the dozen to wade in sunflower seed.

It was my Christmas present, and I can't remember one before or since that has thrilled me as much—not a bicycle or a guitar, a book or a trip.

My father was to make many more feeders, always from found materials—hubcaps and plastic pipes, odds and ends from the warehouse of the pipeline company where he worked. The most elegant piece he produced was a birdbath constructed of a steel pipe welded to an old harrowing disc. Its edges are gently scalloped from wear, and the iron is pitted from decades of immersion. It is the perfect depth for a goldfinch to wade into, the perfect width for a whole family of bluebirds to crowd into. Dad painted it a creamy white to look, as he said, like a destroying angel mushroom, and it does. He showed me how to scrub it out with a lump of sod, soil still attached, scouring away the brown algae. "Dirt cleans pretty well," he used to say. "Your mother wouldn't agree, but it does."

The windowsill feeder finally rotted apart in 1991, and my father died in 1994. When we cleaned out the big house, I got a checkerboard he'd made, a table he'd constructed from an iron sewing machine stand and a plank of fine cherry, an ancient Scots rocker he'd refinished, and the mushroom birdbath. It stands in my front yard, surrounded by flowers, and I still clean it with a lump of sod.

I have a picture of my dad sitting with me on the living room carpet, looking through a great sheaf of Audubon prints he'd gotten for me. He's in an old short-sleeved shirt, the front smeared with grease and oil, varnish and paint from his projects. I'm in heavy black Buddy Holly glasses and short hair, a good look for a hardened tomboy. It's the only picture I have of just us two together, but it speaks volumes about our relationship. Youngest of the five children, I latched onto my

And the turd in the punchbowl, once again, a HY ♀ SSH.

Maybe I'll call her Wild Sally, because she specializes in them.

The mandible's not as deep as I keep trying to make it - in fact I should think of it as a scoop that meets the curve of the maxilla

dad the hardest, followed him around the yard as he gardened, learning his craft seed by seed, weed by weed. I feigned an interest in antique gasoline engines because he would take me out with him, looking for them on long drives through the Virginia countryside. Where there were iron wheels peeking from the weeds, there were bound to be birds, and I wore his old German binoculars' pebbled finish smooth watching them. We became good at evaluating tumbledown sheds for both their machinery and their barn swallow potential.

I am writing this with my three-month-old daughter lounging on a pillow on my lap, her legs hanging off one side as she nurses.

11/3/93

When you get right down to it
this is what bugs me
about illustration and
makes field guide work
impossible for me that need
can't suspend accurate &
to be true.

Finally ready to try foreshortening
after drawing them since Saturday
(It's Wednesday). It makes me
shudder to think how little grasp I have
of the anatomy of the vast majority
of the birds I'm called upon to draw.

She will never know her grandfather, never feel him squeeze her foot, hear him say, "This baby likes to have her foot squeezed"—something he claimed about every baby. He had a soft spot for little girls, as he had for me. I miss him. I realize only now, on becoming a parent, that all the things a child becomes are outgrowths of who her parents are and what they do. I am grateful for all the things he was—farmer, gardener, bird watcher, handyman, teacher, inventor, teller of stories.

I started with grosbeaks, I know. I can't see them without thinking of my father. They come like a memory, unbidden, unexpected, hanging in the bare branches like scattered thoughts. They are beautiful and always welcome, though I always seem to be out of seed when they show up. Every time, I do a one-woman Three Stooges routine upon hearing their calls. I check the feeders—nearly empty. If I don't get the seed out quickly, they might leave. But if I go out to refill the feeders, I will scare them! What to do? Sometimes I hurry out, head down, as if the last thing on my mind is evening grosbeaks. I quickly fill the feeders, then run back to the house. Sometimes I fling handfuls of seed out the window onto the deck. Usually, in trying to welcome them, I wind up scaring them away, and I always panic. I want to see them so badly, want them to stay until the buds swell and the cardinals begin to sing, as they did in the winter of 1967 in Richmond, when I was still my dad's little girl.

A Winter's Tale

FINALLY, I have molted into my winter skin. I have my tea- and hot-cider-making chops back; I've dug my fleece slippers out of the ancient shoe deposits in my closet. I no longer sigh and grimace when I raise the blinds on another layer of gray morning clouds. It's winter, and I am bound to squeeze the beauty and life out of every day, to appreciate what is wonderful about it, and to stop my pointless yearning for the mellow days of autumn past or—perish the thought—the distant warmth of spring.

We're on the edge of the Carolina wren's wintering range. It's a wonderful thing in itself to be in the company of Carolina wrens. Some winters they vanish. An ice storm will knock them back, and their cheerful whistles are heard no more for the next few years. But a pair that's determined to beat the odds is living with us on Indigo Hill this year. We see them frequently at the peanut and suet feeders or prospecting for sunflower bits in the seed litter.

Early on in the winter, every time we went into our garage, a wren spooked out of the shelving and fluttered against the window. We'd hurry to open the garage door and it would always fly out. We'd worry about its getting trapped in there while we weren't around to let it out. This happened so often that I began to suspect that the wrens knew very well how to get in and out of the garage, and the only reason they fluttered against the window was because we were startling

them. This was confirmed when I saw a wren fly from its perch on our old tractor and quietly slip out under the garage door. Now every time we go in, one or two wrens go through this routine.

They're living in there, and better than that, they're sleeping in a new bluebird box that's lying on its side on a high shelf. They've found my mealworm colony and have been rifling through it for the last larvae. They're combing the garage for spiders and crickets, roaches, and who knows what else. Clever birds, those Carolina wrens. On snowy nights when the wind is moaning around the house, I like to think of them snuggled together in their house within a house, making it through the winter with all the accoutrements of man at their disposal.

Depending on your point of view, early November in southern Ohio is wonderful or dreadful. If you enjoy the hunt for deer, it must be wonderful. For me, the best thing about gun season is when it stops. I no longer have to wonder if I look too much like a trophy buck when I trudge to the mailbox, no longer have to drape myself in blaze orange to hang out the clothes. I can resume the little winter rambles that keep cabin fever, with its itchy fingers, at bay. From a high of fourteen deer around the yard last year, we've only three this season. My daughter Phoebe, at four, named the doe Rainbow. She's got twin fawns, a buck and a doe.

Over the summer, I was privileged to see the two fawns at play in the orchard, using my little birch grove outside the studio as a kind of home base. They'd come scatting up the orchard, stop briefly, tongues hanging, at the birch grove, then, with wild leaps and sunfishing, go scalding back down the path. Rainbow would feed, watching idly, as the fawns burned off her good milk in wild play. Gradually their spots faded, and they took on the mien of grown-up deer, with only occasional frisks and flourishes.

As the sun slanted across the meadow on the evening of the last day of gun season, I was delighted to see Rainbow and her two fawns coming up the path. Odd that they'd be abroad in daylight, especially during hunting season, but it was the last day, after all. And they had made it through and would live to see another spring. A good omen.

Suddenly one fawn reared, punched the other with its forefeet, and took off in wild abandon. It rounded the meadow path twice, ears laid back, tail up, bounding and springing like a March hare. As it went by, its mother reared and lashed out with her forelegs, as if to quell its exuberance, but its sibling gave chase. Around and around they frisked, tossing their heads and even play-bowing like pups. The buck folded his front legs, rolled over on his side, and threw his head back as his sister danced up to him, and the chase resumed. Both lapsed into the odd gait called single-footing, when the deer trots, but hops twice on each hoof instead of once. It's as close to skipping as a cervid can come.

Did the three deer know it was the end of the last day of gun season? (They certainly seem to know when it starts! We begin seeing bucks in the orchard just a few days before gun season opens.) Was this a celebration, a party? Undoubtedly. Whatever the deer were celebrating, only they knew. But their joy in simply being alive, whether for the moment or for one more season, was infectious.

This afternoon, as the snow drifted down, Phoebe and I pulled our boots and mittens, hats and coats on and readied ourselves for the quarter-mile walk to the mailbox. Binoculars? Check. Letters? Check. Money for Priority Mail? Check. Jellybeans (in case we get hungry)? Check. I opened the door and Phoebe gasped. "Mommy, it looks just like a coloring book that hasn't been colored on yet!" How perfectly she'd captured the pristine beauty of untrammeled snow. We stood and caught the flakes on our sleeves, looking for a daisy, a star, a double wagon wheel. A Carolina wren mounted the coppery green heron weathervane atop the garage. It bobbed like a little toy, then its clear, happy whistle rang out in the falling snow. Winter? We'll make it through, with a little help from our friends.

frisking in the orchard

Calling Kali

My friend Liz is, I think, a goddess, or perhaps she was one in a previous life. Consider: She's beautiful, wild, creative; she's a botanist and a native plant enthusiast, a bird watcher, artist, teacher. For years she made her living, oddly enough, in a beauty salon, enduring the fumes of nails being lacquered and perms being crimped, dreaming of her next field trip to the measured snip of her scissors. She's more than three-dimensional. Liz sent me a story by Suzin Green about a battle between the gods and the demons in Indian mythology. The demons are winning until the great goddess Durga arrives. When the battle is at its worst, she calls on her most potent aspect, Kali, who leaps from her brow, sweeping like fury itself down on the battlefield, beheading, slaughtering, piles of demon corpses all around her. Unaware that her job is done, she can't stop her bloody dance. If she does not stop, she will destroy the entire world. Durga's consort, Shiva, knows how to appeal to Kali. Taking the form of a tiny infant, he lies down on the battlefield. Kali hears the infant crying in the carnage of bodies, crawls to it, takes it tenderly in her arms, and nurses it, death all around her. A rebirth, so beautiful, from the carnage.

More than a decade ago, Bill and I lived in a rural area of Maryland for a year. It was a strange place, a mix of horse farms, sheep farms, and sprawling new subdivisions. It seemed to me that the three weren't mixing too well, and I mulled over the clash of cultures as I walked the fields and forests.

When I started my afternoon walk, I didn't know that Kali had come along, waiting to leap right out of my brow. The clouds were plump in a rinsed opal sky, and I couldn't bring myself to make a mark on the huge sheet of watercolor paper lying before me. I laced up my boots and started a long, swinging walk out to the meadow. Nearly a mile from home, I stopped at my favorite overlook, searching the sky for the redtail who lives there, counting the cows in the field below. Scanning the familiar landscape, I found a strange lump in a high meadow just over a five-strand fence, a lump that had never been there before. Drawing closer, my horror grew. Two filthy, bloated raccoon carcasses lay spread-eagled, steel traps gripping their mangled feet. Deer legs and viscera lay beside them. A yearling opossum, silvery fur parting in the cold wind, huddled motionless, its hip dislocated by one trap, its shoulder crushed by another. I stepped closer, and it flicked its ear and raised its head painfully, just enough to meet my gaze. On this windswept hill, a crucifixion.

In all, six traps had been set in a ring around the deer entrails, the bait. The coons might have been caught days ago, and they had chewed their feet nearly free before they died of blood poisoning and exposure and sheer agony. The little possum had almost succeeded in chewing her hind foot off. I tried to open the trap holding it and got a blood blister for my efforts. I dreaded what I was going to have to do.

The dry weeds whisked my coat as I loped back up the long trail home. Running into the garage, I seized our wood-splitting maul and a wire cutter and started

back. Another mile rushed by. I was soaked through with sweat, aching from exertion. I squirmed under the barbed wire fence, lifted the maul, and ended the little opossum's misery. As spent and wracked with pain as she was, she died hard, digging little holes in the muddy ground with her good front foot. Blood poured from her mouth. *I'm so sorry, so sorry,* I told her. *This is all I can do for you.* Swearing, crying, I cut the lines anchoring the traps and yanked their pins from the mud. I couldn't free one of the traps clamped on a dead raccoon, so I raised the maul and smashed the iron prison again and again, a message to the farmer's son who had set the traps and then left them untended to do their filthy work.

I hauled the other five traps up and threw them over the fence, along with my maul, and wriggled back under. Taking them into the woods, I smashed them one by one, for they were too heavy to carry home. I hoped, as I beat them into a twisted mass, that they were expensive and wouldn't be replaced. I'd carried out my carnage in full view of the farmer's house. I'd kept an eye on the front door, but I was past caring if anyone came out. I was unrepentant, burning with rage, ready to swing the maul at whoever could do this. I couldn't imagine my neighbor Lester setting these traps. He was a nice man who obviously cared about his cattle. It seemed more a teenage-boy thing to do, to set them and forget them, then come out a week later to kick at the carcasses. I figured they'd been set for coyote, but there never was a song dog born who'd be stupid enough to walk into an amateurish set like this. I imagined a redtail, a turkey vulture, a golden eagle, a beagle, dying in that hideous ring of iron traps, sprawled and stretched and crushed to splinters. I raised the maul over and over, smashing the traps into the ground, then threw some leaves over them and turned for home.

I would go back out in the morning to lug the traps home, to leave little trace of what I'd done. When I thought about it, I realized the right thing to do would have been to trudge down the hill and knock on Lester's door to ask if he was aware of the setup in his pasture. From a property law standpoint, I'd done an awful thing. I'd trespassed; I'd stolen and destroyed someone's property. I was a vandal, but it was a much greater desecration I fought. If I could have helped that little possum, I would have, gathering her in my coat and cleaning her wounds. The Kali image, complete. But I had to kill her, and I had to destroy it all, and I would do it again and again. There are some things that I cannot allow to happen.

I never again crested that hill without seeing the trapped possum in my mind's eye. The vision reminds me that even in the gentlest heart, a potent rage, a powerful destructive force, can lurk. I fill my lungs deeply, send a great cloud of vapor into the frigid air, and walk on, just me and Kali.

The Cursed Tangle

THIS MORNING, for the first time this season, the air was heavy with the sweet scent of maple blossoms. Cloistered as we have been this winter, with both kids trying to get all their childhood illnesses over with in one two-month marathon of coughing, spewing, and sneezing, I have kept my head down, trying to ignore the coming of spring. Winter, with its limited, sad palette, seemed to better fit the mood in the house. Normally, I gather signs of spring like I do the first daffodils; for me, it arrives with the woodcocks in the second week of February.

Starting at 6:39 A.M., a robin sang a long, intricate whisper song under my bedroom window. Huddled into the bones of a trumpet vine, it seemed to sing of placing its mud nest there, once the buds had burst and the sheltering leaves would hide it. I carefully tilted the blinds to look at the bird, which sat, head pulled in, bill closed, wings clamped to its sides, only the slight tremor of its back as evidence that it was singing. Drowsy from a long night of wake-ups, I remembered that it was time for my yearly adjustment to the swelling chorus of birdsong. Since I've been a mother, my hearing is razor-sharp and it never rests, even in slumber. The first song sparrow, tuning up at 5:30, awakens me, and I listen for the bluebird, then the cardinal, then the robin, and finally the house finches and goldfinches and the general rabble of later risers. Ironic as it seems for a bird lover,

robin in trumpet
4/11/05

WINTER 33

I must rely on earplugs and layers of pillows to get any sleep in the morning, until my brain finally learns to start tuning out the birdsong as unimportant, at least when compared to that extra hour of sleep.

Yes, I've been dragging my feet into spring, but today the redbuds were swelling, the color of Harvard beets, nubbins still but full of promise. My walk through the old orchard raised the sharp scent of crushed wild onions, and I noted with pleasure the first blossoms on the small peach whips that have sprouted up around the hollowed carcasses of their elders, once heavy with fruit, now home to beetles, slugs, and the occasional titmouse nest. I walked the borders of the meadow and orchard and noted how much had grown up since Bill and I, in our home-proud fervor eight years earlier, sliced and hacked away the vegetation beneath the ancient apples. It's almost all gone to multiflora rose now, a horrifying prospect to me. Only the heavy, dull blade of the tractor's mower deck keeps it from completely closing over the meadow and orchard.

Multiflora rose is probably the single biggest blob of egg on the tie of the Soil Conservation Service, which introduced it from Asia and sold it to farmers as a "living fence" to be planted along pastures, where it would form an impenetrable tangle that even the strongest Angus could not broach. It wouldn't spread, the SCS assured us, because its seeds had failed to germinate in extensive tests. Those tests failed, however, to include feeding the tiny red rosehips to birds. When scarified, or roughed up, in the gizzards of birds and passed through their digestive tracts, the seeds germinate successfully, wildly, scarily. Multiflora rose carpets the neglected old fields around here, and it is an unwelcome border to all of our open spaces.

Even after multiflora rose and Russian olive, the SCS's enthusiasm for aggressive exotics seems undimmed. An SCS consultant, who was looking over our farm for its pond potential, advised that we plant crown vetch, a carpetlike exotic legume, all around the borders of a potential pond to keep any other vegetation at bay. I looked around at the native little bluestem grass, the pleasant mix of forbs and wildflowers that has come in since we stopped the aggressive mowing schedule kept by the former owners, and wondered at this suggestion. Considering the source, we nodded and changed the subject.

I gaze into the depths of the biggest rose clump, which squats along the border of the meadow behind our house. It's taller than I am, and its branches form an intricate tangle that defines impenetrability. Only a backhoe could root it out now. In the million crisscrosses of its canes are

Multiflora rose
September 19 2005
Really dreadful stuff to handle.
I'm all full of holes with just
these sprigs!

countless spangles of white, the droppings of all the birds that find shelter in this hedge. Each autumn it produces a galaxy of hips, to be spread far and wide by the same birds. It's a monster factory.

And yet . . . when the sharp-shinned hawk zips through the yard, its talons ready for the slow and the sick, where do the birds dive? When the snows of winter come horizontally, where do the cardinals huddle? Where do the towhee and the song sparrow clamber and sing? Looking through the canes, I see the flat platforms of several old cardinal nests, trimmed in dried grape tendrils. A catbird nest is bulkier, woven of grape bark and twigs. Up higher, in the next clump, the cantaloupe-sized mass of sticks that sheltered our beloved brown thrashers hangs. Field sparrows weave their delicate blond baskets in the smaller multiflora shrubs that have avoided the mower for a season or two. I know the yellowthroats and prairie warblers nest here, too, though I've never been able to find their constructs. And along the driveway I heard the lusty calls of a near-fledging brood of yellow-breasted chats issuing from another monster clump.

If you could ask the birds about the merits of this noxious exotic, you would get a different answer than I would give. I have to grant multiflora rose, however grudgingly, a high mark for usefulness to wildlife, even as I know it crowds out the black raspberry and sumac that really belong here. Much as I would like to wish it away, I can't; I can't even begin to hack it away. The long canes retaliate, hooking into my back and neck, tearing my skin. It's like fighting a Ninja octopus. Like the European starling, the house sparrow, like Japanese honeysuckle and tree of heaven, it's here to stay, whether we like it or not, and I have to look at it as the birds do. Multiflora rose is a permanent part of the picture on our farm, and we'll try to keep it in check as best we can. More important, we'll try to look at it through a cardinal's eyes, as a curse that is at least part blessing.

The Generous Robin

WHEN YOU walk the same route every few days, each walk becomes a separate entity, has a personality and presence all its own. Some are a little bland, some plain but sporting a diamond cufflink, and some just burst out of every seam with drama and life. Such was today's walk.

I've walked the Loop so many times in the last eleven years that I've worn a little trail. The sharp hooves of deer and tridents of wild turkey cut their own patterns over my boot prints. The animals seem to approve when I clip away the briers and sumac to clear my path each fall. The first snowfall reveals the traffic, from deer to fox to coyote, to bobcat, skunk, and grouse. Everyone, it seems, appreciates a good trail. If I really need to hustle, I can walk the Loop in a half hour, but it takes forty-five minutes to appreciate much. If I see things and stop for them, an hour flies by and I don't even realize it.

I hear the distant laughter of migrating robins, February robins, spreading springtime through the bare twigs. They come back just when I need them most, the vanguard of spring's delights. As I draw close to my high overlook, their giggling grows louder and suddenly they are everywhere, swooping down into the cow pasture, their erect forms and neat flat heads punctuating its nascent green fuzz. It is a mixed flock, with as many females as males. I wish I'd thought to bring a sketch pad. Their wings hang low at their sides, looking more like a pair of

9/27/95
in the dead oak
Scolding: Robin
Cape May
Scarlet Tanager
Pacific jays

crutches, really, than wings. They seem to balance the birds like arms as the robins make swift stabs into the softening earth, coming up with a worm for almost every stab.

I remember a range map I've seen for the American robin. Red—for breeding—blankets almost all of North America except the desert Southwest, where, I realize, the soil is too dry and sandy for earthworms. Such a hearty, lovely bird, and it has followed us, our well-watered lawns, our imported fescues and imported earthworms, wherever we've gone. It's a bird that is at home in deep woods, yet finds nearly ideal conditions in our cookie-cutter suburbs. I wonder where these scores of robins are headed. Would that one make for the cool forests of Cape Breton? Would another weave its nest in a crab apple next to the loudspeaker at the fast-food drive-through in town? How I would love to know.

A constant soft chorus of song

spreads through the woods, riddled with their *keep-keep* notes and soft, sudden laughter—*tee Hee hee hee*. It is a bird party, and it's all coming from the woodland edge; the foraging birds are silent. More and more robins swoop down until I count seventeen in one sweep of my binoculars. There are dozens more in the woods, keeping watch.

Reluctantly, I get to my feet and push onward. Much as I'd have liked to watch robins all day in the warming February wind, I have a school bus to meet. Stepping carefully down the steep slope I call the Chute, I pause at the spot that's marked by a spent shotgun shell. I almost always see a grouse here, which helps explain the shell casing—a hunter once did, too. Though I pick up trash when I find it, I like to see that red shell because it reminds me that a lucky grouse still lives here and that other people sometimes walk this land, use my paths with quite different intent from mine.

Today, a strange bird takes awkward flight from the magic spot—a young male sharp-shinned hawk. He flies low and clumsily, the carcass of a largish bird dangling beneath him. I kneel and pick up some wing feathers, a leg picked to the bone—a robin. The toes are soft and pliable; it has been killed within the hour. I scan the underbrush and find the hawk once again bent over its kill, tearing away bites with twists of his small sharp bill. He eyes me briefly and decides to go on with his meal. I look at the feathers in my hand. He had caught a hen robin. Five, ten, maybe fifteen turquoise eggs that would never be laid, this season or any, orange diamond mouths that would never

"*Whenever a man hears it, he is young, and Nature is in her spring; wherever he hears it, it is a new world and a free country, and the gates of heaven are not shut against him.*"

—Thoreau

pop open. And yet, it's a big meal for a small sharp-shin. There are plenty of robins, and some are meant for hawks. The tinge of sadness evaporates, and I lay the robin's foot and feathers on the ground next to the red shotgun shell.

Using his bill like a scissors, the sharpie cuts away the robin's synsacrum and femur, freeing a large zigzag morsel that is mostly bone. Three times he tries to choke it down, until I realize that I am most likely the cause of his undue haste. I take the hint and quietly move on, leaving him to eat in peace. Still the robins chuckle in the woods, their day only momentarily perturbed by the loss of a flock mate.

I push on to climb the steep grassy hill I call the Cut, where a natural gas line makes a slash through our oak-hickory forest. A robin's song, separate and all the more beautiful in its simplicity, rings through the hollow. I stop to rest and listen. The roiling gray sky tells of rain. I catch the scent of maple flowers on the warm breeze, hear a robin's simple song, and the whole spring just rolls out behind my closed eyes like a carpet, and I am in my mind's eye sleeveless and sweating and planting peas, then beans, and even tomatoes. I'm picking zinnias and hanging my feet in the fishpond and making pesto. Life seems so full of possibility, drenched with anticipation of the magic to come. Like Thoreau listening to a wood thrush, I am young again, and all Nature is in her spring.

I think of the sharp-shin, now finishing his meal in a tangle of grapevines and plucked feathers. He is full again, and Nature is in her spring. We're glad the robins are back.

SPRING

Giving a convincing pileated call, his wings going flup-flup-flup, he flies right across my path as if being yanked on a string; he dances like a yellow yo-yo. His wings seem to stay up the whole time over his back. I don't see how he stays aloft.

Then perches with a How-do-you-like-that look. Does he remember when I whistled at him and he tried to hit me in the head?

Off-seasons

Skulking from nest

IT IS THE OFF-SEASONS I love the most; almost any naturalist does. The beach in early spring, swept clean by winter storms, only the barest hint of green at the base of the dune grass clumps. A piping plover, like the pale ghost of a semi-palmated plover, runs, stops, freezes, pipes its plaintive note. It has just arrived on a March warm front, though the day holds no warmth. Here it will stay, and dig its shallow cup in the sand, and lay its precious chocolate-flecked khaki eggs among the shell bits. On the clean spring beach, there is hope and life beginning.

Visit the same beach in July, if you dare, and thread your way past the rows of parked cars and through the blare of radios and scent of cocoa butter, weave your way through the prone human bodies strewn about the sand, and try to believe it is the same beach you tramped alone in March. Look for the piping plovers, but they are gone. Were they able to bring off their young, windblown balls of thistle-down, before the crowds descended? You marvel that piping plovers still exist in this scenario. Yes, it is the off-seasons I love most.

Every spring, along about late March, a silent alarm sounds in my heart for the arriving plovers. While working for The Nature Conservancy, I created the flagship

program to protect them along the Connecticut coastline, putting up string fencing and educational signs to fence off the vital beach nesting areas used by plovers and least terns. I'd sniff the air rushing by in the first big warm front of March and know they had arrived. I'd drive down to the coast and hit all eight or ten nesting areas, and there they would be, twinkling over the low dunes and down by the lapping wavelets of Long Island Sound. Even as I tried to predict where they might settle and planned the massive effort of protecting their nesting areas, they ran energetically over the sand, the embodiment of undimmed hope.

Certainly, one would have to be an optimist to lay one's precious eggs on the sand of a busy Connecticut beach, where the day patrol of seminude bodies and romping dogs gives way to a night shift of skunks, rats, cats, and red foxes. For those three seasons, from 1983 to 1986, I felt a great weight of responsibility to protect them, and I walked the flesh off my bones lugging heavy signposts to the remote beaches where they chose to nest. I don't recognize myself in pictures from that time. My cheeks are hollow; my clothes hang loosely on me.

Mingling with fishermen, sunbathers, jet skiers, the curious, and the simply nasty, I spread a strange gospel of tolerance and caring to people who had no idea such birds existed, even as plovers and terns ran past their feet and flew over their heads. "How could there be birds nesting here?" I was asked. "There aren't any trees!" I relieved one well-meaning family of its brood of least tern chicks, carefully gathered up into a picnic basket to be taken home, but I never was able to catch the people who gathered and ate the tern and plover eggs every spring at a little beach below Bridgeport. It was a time best looked back upon from the remove of having done it and then moved on.

And yet, March comes, and this little bell goes off, and I catch a certain scent even on the Ohio wind, so very far from the coastline. I remember those after-

noons of heavy gray skies and leaden waves and tiny pale birds, when almost all I had to worry about were plovers and terns. Conservation efforts such as the one I created often run on the bright, hot fuel of the young and caring. More often than not, it is women who take up the cause of these fragile beach nesters, who are moved enough by their plight to act. Some might label it a misdirected maternal instinct; whatever it is, it is a potent force for good, and the women conservationists I came to know were like a pride of lionesses, willing to stop at nothing to protect their charges.

At the time, blinded by the need to act, I couldn't understand why I had so

much trouble scraping up even a handful of volunteers who'd help when that need was so obvious to me. Now, as three-year-old Phoebe pads into the room and climbs onto my lap, and I hear four-month-old Liam awakening too early from his afternoon nap, I understand.

We become entangled in the gentle mesh of family life, in the need to rise from a warm bed four and five times during a night to fill a tummy or smooth a brow, to be home for nurturing of our own young. The young of plovers and terns must fend for themselves. And I say a silent prayer of thanks for the next student, fresh from wildlife management courses, who takes on the job of trying to protect them. It is a constantly revolving door, for only a very few people last more than a year or two at such a strenuous and occasionally disheartening job.

Off-seasons—I am in one now, when I must stay close to home, anchored by naptimes, mealtimes. Cabin fever prowls around my mind, rubbing its lean sides on my psyche. I find myself thinking of small pale birds and porcelain eggs among the shell bits, and wondering who is taking care of them now.

Phoebe Magic

IT WAS THE PHOEBE NEST
that did it, that made us willing
to do anything to buy this property. I'm sure the seller saw it in our
eyes. That worn little lump of moss and
mud, plopped atop a pressure-treated two
by-eight beneath the house's raised deck,
upped our ante clear to heaven. Yes, he told us, phoebes had nested there just that
summer, and their cat had had a marvelous time watching the birds through the
flooring as it crouched directly above them. I smiled and suppressed a scream—
both Bill and I had gotten good at that in our nine months of till now fruitless
house hunting in southeast Ohio. Searching for a rural property, we'd seen it all.
Beautiful pieces of land with houses that begged not for repair but only to be
bulldozed. Beautiful homes, with shiny new kitchens, that shook with each passing semi truck or had embarked on a slow death march down an eroding
hill. There was a fairly decent old farmhouse adjoining a state forest, where the
neighbor boys staged a three-ring all-terrain vehicle extravaganza for our benefit.
Rrrrrrrrrr, yahoo!

And now here was this house, a pretty good house, on forty acres of meadow, orchard, and forest, with another forty waiting to be bought, and it had the ultimate lucky sign—a nest of one of our very favorite birds right under the deck. As we walked the close-shaven meadow, I'd found a couple of bleached box turtle shells, victims of a too-low mower deck and a too-enthusiastic mowing schedule. We'd fix that. There were problems, to be sure, with the water supply, the kitchen, the baths, and the floor plan—the stuff of future home-improvement loans. For us, in that moment of discovery, the old farm with its hastily built, 1978-vintage house shone with perfection.

That was the autumn of 1992. We moved in that December. The phoebe nest melted away in the winter rains, and every spring thereafter a phoebe came, sometimes for a day or two, sometimes for only a couple of hours, sang its cranky, wheezy song, and flew away. It would be seven years before a phoebe pair nested there again. We put up little three-sided shelters under the deck and eaves and lay low whenever a phoebe appeared to investigate. If crossed fingers made eggs, we'd be overrun with phoebes.

As I write, there is a phoebe muttering and fluttering under the deck. He's been on our territory for over a week. He sits on the railing, wagging his tail and whisking up to nab sluggish houseflies against the south-facing siding. It's the longest a phoebe has ever lingered here. I pretend to ig-

nore him. It's best he not know how much I want him to find a mate and build a nest. I'll even make mud for him, run a hose into my flower bed, if he'll just be so kind as to slap it on a deck strut, line it with moss, and get busy.

He starts singing at a few minutes after seven in the morning, starts earlier every day, and he always wakes me up. I don't mind. There's something about this drab little flycatcher that I love unreservedly. To me, a phoebe embodies bird spirit, that charge of life that one bird can bring to an otherwise dull day. He's always in motion, even at rest, flopping his loose-hinged tail, then whirling off to catch a flying insect. His magic has nothing to do with color; he defines drab, without even a wing bar or eye ring for relief from his brownness. But look in a phoebe's eye and it's all there: the charm of a warbler, the zest of a kingbird. He's a lot of bird in deceptively plain packaging.

We have a friend, Larry, of whom we're very fond and who lives not far from here. As long as he's lived in these Appalachian foothills, he's used guns to fell food and occasionally to settle disputes. One was with a phoebe, who came one spring to put globs of wet mud atop a porch light by Larry's front door. I wish I had a story of revelation and redemption to tell, but I don't. The phoebe lost. I think our friend made a mistake there, but perhaps the bigger mistake was in ever telling us what he'd done. I guess I have a skewed outlook on phoebes, because it would never occur to me to consider the inevitable mess beneath their nests an annoyance, much less a death sentence. It goes part and parcel with the joy of having phoebes around. But then, I once climbed into my landlord's garage rafters and hung an old umbrella upside down under a barn swallow nest, to save his truck from their fallout and spare them any possible consequences of his annoyance. Barn swallows, like phoebes, are worth it. Watch swallows skim low over the lawn in the sidelight of a summer evening; watch a phoebe whirl out to snap up a passing crane fly, then fetch up on a dead branch, and then imagine the scene without their spark.

When our daughter was born, she had the spark in her eyes. As a tiny newborn, she'd whip around when anyone entered the room and track them, holding their eyes in her smoky blue gaze. She still has them, nearly ten years later, those wise eyes. An old soul, someone once said. Before I knew she was a girl, before she ever came, she had a name: Phoebe. It had belonged to a great-aunt of mine, I was told after we'd picked it. *That's nice*, I thought, *but it's really the bird I'm naming her for.* Everyone knew that. Phoebe draws with me in the studio, picks bundles of zinnias, writes outrageous stories complete with illustrations. I can't imagine the house without her spark. Together, we root for the lone male phoebe, hoping he'll attract a mate with his itchy song. House deal, firstborn's name—how can a person base such momentous decisions on a nondescript little flycatcher? You'd have to know the phoebe.

Mowing the Meadow

GRACE VISITS OFTEN when you live deep in the country, but she seems to come around more than usual in April. I spend the month in a state of building ecstasy as one wonderful thing after another unfolds, each a fresh surprise yet old as time. The ringing song of a newly arrived brown thrasher on a misty morning makes me laugh out loud, especially when I have the peas and lettuce planted the night before he arrives. *Pick it up, pick it up, drop it, drop it, cover it, cover it!* he exhorts, and I can smile smugly, because I already have.

Managing these eighty acres boils down to a constant struggle to keep the twelve that are open, open. It's a pitched battle with multiflora rose and Japanese honeysuckle and a horrid plumy exotic *Miscanthus* grass that escaped from bouquets at a little church cemetery about a mile away. Mow, and everything backs down for a year or two. Let it slide, and mowing becomes brush hogging, becomes forestry.

Complicating this battle plan are the innocents in the middle, the birds that like things a bit overgrown, a little brushy. We leave last summer's growth standing in the meadow over the winter for all the juncos and sparrows that need the seeds and cover. Traditionally our mowing season begins in early spring, when it gets warm enough for Bill to think about tinkering with our '54 Massey-Ferguson

Field Sparrow gathers "straws - April
"Cat's whiskers"

tractor in the cold garage. It ends when we see the first field sparrow sporting cat's whiskers of pale grasses on her way to a nest under construction. In cold, wet springs like this one, those two parameters collide.

Last year, we added another constraint when Bill's first, second, and third mowing passes along the east border put up a woodcock from the same spot. Our suspicions of a nest were confirmed when, a few weeks later, I found in the same spot a nearly whole, freshly pipped eggshell, lavender-splotched, too big for any songbird. It had the distinctive pyriform shape of a shorebird egg, the only shorebird that displays, mates, and nests on our property. I was ecstatic.

So it was a nudge from grace, I believe, that sent me out onto the deck to check Bill's progress as he mowed the meadow on a Sunday afternoon. Liam, three and a half, bundled in two coats and a yellow stocking hat, was supervising from the deck, waving and calling to his daddy as Bill rounded the near corner. Suddenly, a big, fawn-colored bird rose practically from under the mower deck and flew erratically a few yards to the edge of the woods, where it landed. A woodcock! Bill couldn't have seen it; he'd already passed when it flew up. I marked the spot in my mind and sprinted toward him to keep the tractor from making another pass. Bill turned off the tractor and we searched the area together. We found no eggs, but the ground nest of a woodcock is so beautifully camouflaged that we chalked it up to poor searching. Bill left the narrow, unmown strip as it was and called it a day.

The next morning, I got up early and walked quietly out to the meadow, scanning the unmown strip. There she was, still as a rock, hunkered down into the wet grass between two small multiflora rosebushes. Her onyx eyes and the black bar across her high, angular forehead had given her away. I caught my breath. The world buzzed and sang around me. A couplet from Margaret Gibson's heartbreakingly beautiful poem "Gift" sprang into my mind.

Yes
I had wanted to rest—but rest
is just this quiet
tumult in the body's
own blossom, that turns the sky
to avalanche, and ocean.

The mower deck had missed her nest by eight inches. On the next pass, the
tractor wheel would have rolled right over the eggs. She had stood her ground as

April 16 4:30 pm
She's still on the nest.
We discovered it April 6 and
she was sitting tight
until the mower deck passed 8" away
She sank lower as I drew until she was
barely visible. Note wing position- young?

April 14 1994

the huge red machine had roared up and past her, rising off her eggs only when
the shrapnel-spewing deck practically touched her. Now she would have to finish
out their incubation in this narrow strip of brush, a feature in the now-featureless
mown meadow. The multiflora around her was leafing out rapidly, though, and for
once I was thankful for its rampant growth.

I left her to her silent work and walked back home, thinking about the irony
of land management. If we didn't mow, the woodcocks would have no place to
stage their displays or lay their eggs. Yet our mowing was the single greatest threat
to their reproductive success. Every way I thought about it, I met a blind corner.
We'd always mown in patches, the worst first, as we put it. The best answer I
could come up with was to mow only half the meadow each spring and to do it
earlier yet, before the woodcocks had settled on a nest site. We'd just have to put
up with a ragged-looking meadow. What's the point of managing a meadow for
breeding woodcocks if you wind up smashing their nests?

Though it's still really too cold and early to do much, I find something to do in the garden every evening. Bill tilled it for me, and I've got the snap peas and the lettuce and mustard green seeds planted. I'm trying to stay ahead of the weeds, knowing I'll lose. I let them go to seed every fall, because the indigo buntings and sparrows flock in to rustle around in the wreck of my garden, feasting on goosefoot and foxtail seeds, and I love to be greeted with the whir of their wings when I open the gate.

Mostly, though, I time things so I'm in the garden alone when the woodcock begins to call. Starting at dusk, his funny raspberry call bursts across the meadow. He *peent*s twenty, thirty times, then launches slowly into the air, wings twittering, in a huge swinging circle over our house. So high now he looks like an aspen leaf, he suddenly sideslips, falling to earth in jagged zags, singing like mad the whole time—a liquid twitter that falls like silver rain all around me. I stand in the dark, heart swelling. *Your children are safe*, I tell him. *Make some more, will you?*

Six Gifts of April

IT's A GIFT DAY, like a birthday, when I am showered with nice things. *Oh, stop, you shouldn't have!* I always wish I could space them out through the year, for those cold, gray mornings when I could really use a present. The gifts today are so simple and small that they might go unnoticed by many people, yet they're riches untold to me.

FIRST GIFT: It's warm, and the sun is shining. Spring has been dragging her dress through the cold mud this year, meandering, seemingly simpleminded and without purpose. Will she ever arrive? The trees are in a holding pattern; only the maples have their red flowers. Even the birches, usually so impetuous and ready to put on their pale green party dresses, are barely budded. Daffodils and pussy willows have gone on ahead, as is their wont, but all the others seem to be waiting for poor, errant Spring. Today should help remind her that she has work to do.

*Narcissus "Salome"
the last one standing in
my garden—and more
lovely as it ages
April 19, 2005*

SECOND GIFT: Tree swallows have arrived, kiting around the big meadow, diving on the housebound bluebirds, seeming to mock them with their superior flying prowess. I'm glad they're late; I won't have to worry about them through so many freezing nights. The male who nested in our martin gourds last year sat on a low-hanging telephone wire and cocked his head when I walked right under him and spoke to him. He didn't leave, didn't even interrupt his jingly twitter. I can't be sure it's the same bird, of course, but he's sitting in the same place and he's ridiculously tame, and that's enough for me. Gift received.

THIRD GIFT: The chipping sparrows are back this morning—the first birds I saw when I opened my eyes, a pair was pecking about in the old messy flower bed under the bedroom window. Chipping sparrows have snuck up on me in their gentle, understated way, shouldering aside a number of other candidates to be near the top of my list of favorite yard birds. They seem to appreciate me, too. I've had them court and mate within a few feet of where I stood, riveted. They never fail to find and accept the special foods I offer them: mealworms, rolled oats, peanuts, sunflower hearts, and crushed eggshells. I find their color scheme, with their neat ruddy berets, white eyebrows, and clean gray underparts, very fetching. And their small, beautifully woven nests, invariably lined with my hair, are enchanting. They're fully worth the slight embarrassment I feel when I ask the puzzled beautician for my floor sweepings.

FOURTH GIFT: A mockingbird showed up out of nowhere today and fluttered around the yard, singing at about half power, but singing. For those who are inundated with mockingbirds, this may seem like no big deal, but I have learned over the years that you have to live without such birds to truly appreciate them. Tree swallows, chipping sparrows, mockingbirds: Relocations from Virginia to Massachusetts to Connecticut to Maryland to Ohio have left me bereft of them for years at a time. Meeting up with them again is all the sweeter. Mockingbirds are scarce way out here in the country, almost an event. We don't as yet have the variety of fruit-bearing ornamental shrubs and trees they need to last the winter, though we're working on it. A few pass through in spring, pinwheeling around the yard with their white wing patches flashing, singing. Hearing them, I am a child again, waking up on a sum-mer midmorning in Virginia to the drone of lawnmowers and the song of mockingbirds.

All her whites are dirty Shes like a bag of old rumpled laundry

FIFTH GIFT: An adult male yellow-bellied sapsucker appeared in one of my gray birches this morning. He drilled three small holes and spent about twenty minutes hopping from one to the other. I could see the thin, clear birch sap glistening in the sun as he lapped it up. I love my nine gray birches, now eight years old and six to eight inches through the trunk. Despite their name, their bark is snow white. I planted them because they have always been my favorite trees and because they remind me of New England. They've just gotten big enough to attract a sapsucker, it seems. I've got mixed feelings. I saw what sapsuckers did to my father's sad little pecan trees in Virginia. I hope they don't love my birches to death! For now, I'll drink in his beauty, pale lemon, bloodred, black, and white, as he drinks my trees' sap. Good thing I planted six more yesterday!

SIXTH GIFT: Bluebirds are building a nest in the slot box in the front yard, a nest of flax stems.

I had a revelation while clearing the vegetable garden of last year's dead stalks. As I was cutting back the bushel basket–sized tops of the perennial flax plants, I noticed that their stems were very fine, but fibrous, springy, and strong. I couldn't break them off; I had to find my sharpest shears to cut them. Commercially, flax is grown to make linen. I grow perennial flax for the airy drifts of sky blue flowers that light up my garden all summer. But I think I've found an even higher use. Chopping the flax tops into five-inch lengths, I took a trash can full of fine gray stems and tucked them into a large suet feeder, leaving little piles out on the grass for the bluebirds to find. What satisfaction to find them incorporated into the bluebirds' nest foundation the same afternoon! I'll be watching to see if the field and chipping sparrows approve as well.

As I think about it, I realize that none of this is coincidence. Gifts are bestowed, yes, but not without good reason: We've done what we can to welcome these birds into our habitat, putting out nest boxes for the bluebirds and gourds for the tree swallows, planting shrubs and trees for the mockingbird and sapsucker, setting out delicacies and nesting material for the chipping sparrows. With a start, I realize that none of these birds were here when we arrived on the property in 1992. I remember something Bill said in 1991, when we first considered a move to Ohio. "Don't worry. Wherever we end up, we'll make our own weather." And so, it seems, we have.

The Planting Bird

I CAN'T REMEMBER a spring when I wasn't ready to embrace it, meet it head-on. Maybe it's because we've all been sick since early February; maybe it's the long-term sleep deprivation that comes as part of the package with a new baby. Maybe it's the five woodchucks that had their way with my vegetable garden all last summer. They showed the way to eleven deer, and the sixteen of them laid waste to everything. The mesclun lettuce mix went first, chewed to the ground. Though their leaves were too prickly to eat, the zucchini and summer squash fruits were eagerly consumed. The tomato plants and their fruit simply disappeared. Even the jalapeños were reduced to naked stems festooned with cheery green and red peppers. My plans for making Sungold Salsa as a Christmas present for my extended family withered with the drought and the animal onslaught. The garden, started with such high hopes, looked as though someone had taken a weed whacker to it. I couldn't even get a salad out of it.

By midwinter, I was finally ready to order that eight-foot-high antideer mesh, ready to sink almost $500 into protecting a meager sixteen-by-thirty-two-foot garden. I didn't want to calculate the cost per tomato; I'd already spent so much on soil and lumber for the raised beds, on four-foot-high fencing to stop the rabbits and woodchucks (the latter blithely climbed it). No, the garden makes no economic sense whatsoever, and I know that. But I can't put a value on being able to plant and grow my own fresh produce, to be free, at least for a couple of months, of the dismal, chemical-drenched, tasteless provender stacked in grocery bins. To walk out of a summer evening and stuff myself with sugar snap peas, to fill the front of my shirt with little tangerine-colored Sungold tomatoes, to toss them into a bowl of hot pasta coated with my own pesto and call it dinner—that is something beyond price.

I still couldn't look at the garden plot, though, marred as it was with deer tracks and the stubs of last year's plants. So when an April Saturday came with a

Buttercrunch
April 19 2005
It's so dry I'll have to water
again today. Tough spring
for frogs and lettuce.

balmy breeze laced with the scent of blooming red maples and wet earth, I climbed atop our bird watching tower and faced west, away from the garden plot. It was too depressing to think about. And a song drifted up from the old orchard, of notes in pairs, seemingly distant yet curiously close: *Pick it up, pick it up. Drop it, drop it. Cover it, cover it.* The brown thrasher was back. My father always told me he was the planting bird. He came when it was time to plant peas, and he told you how to do it.

I swiveled my scope onto the hidden thrasher and drank him in. He had a rusty back, pure burnt sienna; a gray cheek; a long, strong bill; an eye the color of egg yolk. He sat still, tail drooping, turning his head mechanically, sending out his message. And I felt my blood stir and begin to reach my weary brain. It was time to plant the peas. I laughed aloud and hurtled down the stairs to find my work gloves.

Tearing into last year's stalks, I pulled all the old plants out of the ground and piled them in the middle of the plot. In a ritual as old as time, I touched a match to them and stepped back to watch the flame flicker, catch, then roar, cleaning out the old to make way for the new. The smoke rolled up, blue and thick, and the flames sang as they reached for the sky. I poked and raked and watched until last year's failures were reduced to white ash. The sweet smoke stung my nose as it rolled heavenward.

Next, I went to the garage for the garden plow that had belonged to my German grandmother, Frieda Ruigh. I never look at the plow without seeing her, wearing hose, a flowered dress, and beat-up pumps, pushing it through the rich, dark soil of her Iowa garden. I see her digging new potatoes for the noonday meal, picking strawberries, still in that dress. She's been gone now for twenty-eight years, but sometimes I still miss her, her thick accent, her dancing eyes and wry smile, so much that I cry.

Sugar snaps coming
up April 19, 2005

The plow—such a wellspring of memories. My thoughts shift to my father,
who dug it out of Frieda's garage when she could no longer use it. He refinished it
and painted the metal parts John Deere green. When the time came for him to
give up his garden, he told me to take it, and as much as I hated to think of his
never using it again, I did. Everything I know about gardening I learned at his side.
For the first few years, it was mostly weeding, until I took over everything but the
planting. He always accused me of watering too much, even as he'd remark on
how juicy and tender the tomatoes and beans were. It was the perfect apprentice-
ship. He got to plant his garden, and he had a willing helper to weed, water, tend,
and harvest it. And he made me a woman of the soil, just like Frieda. He's gone
now, too, but I see his hands and hear his voice in my mind as I tend my own
garden.

Frieda's plow has a little iron wheel out in front, five sharp recurved tines, and a foot brace. You situate yourself between the long arms of the plow, put your foot on the brace, and go, kind of hop-stepping as you push it with both arms and one leg. Ergonomic it is not; the handles are clumsy and the plow depth adjuster sticks up just enough to give you a nickel-sized bruise on your shin as you push it forward. But it does a fine job of loosening the soil and uprooting weeds. I revel in the stands of still-tiny goosefoot that fall before its little blades, thinking of my dad's admonition: "The time to get weeds is while they're small." How true! Left to mature, each of those goosefoot plants would get a taproot and a woody stem. I'd need two hands to pull them within a few weeks. Leave goosefoot to grow and before you know it, you won't be able to pull it up at all.

Two hours flew by under the warm March sun as I burned and plowed and dug a troweled trench along the back side of the garden. The paper-dry peas rolled from my fingers into the furrow, and I planted a few extra on the side to dig up, so I could check on the progress of their germination. Over the next two weeks, they'd swell and soften, send out a root, and finally raise green heads to the sky. A rumble of thunder sounded, and I looked up to see fine white thunderheads piling up against the soft blue sky. Great splashing raindrops sluiced down on me, and I sprinted to the garage doorway to breathe in the fresh ozone smell and watch the soil darken with moisture. *Pick it up, pick it up. Drop it, drop it. Cover it, cover it . . .* The planting bird began to sing again. I had let a bird tell me how to spend my Saturday, and that was just fine with me.

Weary but happy, I came back into the house and laid my work gloves on a side table. My eyes fell on a framed photograph, one of only two I have of my grandmother Frieda Ruigh. The year is 1974, and she is making a rare visit from her tiny hometown in Iowa to our family in Virginia. It is her eightieth birthday. She is

smiling, wearing the hairnet she always wore, and there are two lines of pink rouge high above her cheekbones. Next to her is a painting pushed into a photo frame, the kind with the cardboard triangle behind it that makes it stand up. It is my first real bird painting, the first to find its way into a frame, and I have painted it for her because it is her favorite bird. She would sit down on the stoop to listen to its song whenever she heard it. The art is primitive, to be sure, with a made-up rosebush for a perch, but it is rendered with the care and conviction of a sixteen-year-old who knows she'll paint birds for a living someday. It is a brown thrasher, and it is singing.

A Bad Day for Starlings

It's April 15. Spring is unfolding into summer. Everything's happening at once now. The black-and-white warbler is singing his wheezy lay from the orchard, tiger swallowtails are bouncing all over the yard, the lilac perfumes the warm breeze. Toads whir and trill in the fishpond, grappling and turning over and over in an ecstasy of sex and war. We finally decide to oust the starlings from our beautiful, expensive, state-of-the-art cluster of purple martin nesting gourds. Bill cranks the set down its aluminum pole and I set about cleaning the straw from all eight. The starlings, two pairs, have had trouble deciding which gourd to settle in. I amuse myself by sorting through the nesting materials. Mostly it's stem sheaths from the ornamental *Miscanthus* grasses around the yard. But in one nest, there's a mushy jalapeño pepper from last summer's crop, and in another, a freshly picked, butter yellow miniature narcissus flower. The pepper makes me laugh; the flower makes me groan. There's a birdy aesthetic operating here, and I feel like a heel to be destroying their careful creations.

The last nest I clean has four pale blue starling eggs in it. Two have been punctured and two are addled, infertile, the yolks without form. Another lies shattered on the ground below the nest. The vicious fights I've witnessed between two of the nesting starlings must have stemmed from the egg piracy. I hadn't known that

Starlings arguing over
our martin gourds

SPRING 77

starlings would throw each other's eggs out. Their fights had been impressive, with both birds butting chests on the ground, standing as tall as possible, singing at the top of their lungs as they grappled and rolled. Even without my intervention, no young starlings would have come from this clutch.

All the gourds are clean, and we place duct tape over their entrances to further discourage the starlings until the martins we hope for start to show up around the first of May. We've never had more than passing interest from purple martins, but we hope that this new set of gourds will attract them this year. Undaunted by the duct tape over their gourd entrances, the two male starlings continue to mix it up on the ground beneath the pole.

I'm inside the house a couple of hours later when I hear a sound like tearing cloth, the whoosh of hawk wings, followed by agonized cries from one of the starlings. Rounding the corner of the house, I spook an immature sharp-shinned hawk, who's struggling to subdue his feisty meal among my tulips and larkspur. He lumbers into the air, then lands hard in a clump of multiflora rose. It sounds like someone threw a rock into the bushes. I leave him alone and run to get Bill and the spotting scope. The starling is still yelling. What a way to go.

Years ago, I found a small, immature male sharp-shin in the same predicament. He'd nabbed a starling, but he couldn't quite kill it, nor could he fly off with it. Every time he bent his head to try to administer the coup de grace, the starling would stab at his eyes. He kept shifting his grip and almost losing his prey. Two hours later, he finally was able to eat. This hawk was more experienced, and it wasn't long before the piteous cries stopped and he began to feed. After he left, I worked my way into the rose clump to recover the bright yellow bill parts of the starling to show to Bill and Phoebe. There's something poignant about these scattered feathers and bits of what was only this morning a scrappy, singing, vibrant bird. Still, I'm glad the sharp-shin had a meal, of an introduced exotic no less.

When I was young and less wise, I accepted a nearly fledged starling from an acquaintance, who had raised it and named it Einstein. Though I knew I shouldn't, I trained it for soft release, teaching it to come when called and feed from special dishes that I placed around my yard. It was a grand little bird, with only a couple of annoying habits. It would perch on my shoulder and insert its long pointed bill in my ear, then open its mandibles, as if to spread the ear canal wider. Ouch! Given half a chance, it would do the same maneuver in a nostril, which was even more disconcerting. I got the feeling the bird enjoyed the startled reaction it got from me each time it attempted this. Watch starlings feeding on a lawn and you'll see the same behavior. The closed bill is inserted in the sod, and strong masseter muscles force the bill open to create a hole and expose its insect prey.

I liked Einstein. He made me laugh. The day I released him, he appeared on my studio windowsill with a nickel in his bill and tapped it on the window. Trying to buy his way back into the house? I went outside with a few mealworms for him and he dropped the nickel in my hand. You have to love a bird that pays for what it gets.

Still thinking about starlings, I head for my twice-weekly trip to town to provision the house and run a few errands. A starling sits on a wire on busy Acme Street, and I watch him as I wait at a red light. He flies down to a spot in the middle of the road, walks around with that curious, potbellied strut, neck craned at something that lies in the road. Food? The traffic thickens and roars up, and the bird rises back up to the wire, only to drop down again, walking tight circles around the object. My car nears, and my heart sinks to see that the bundle in the road is another starling, just killed. Fearless, the starling dodges trucks and cars to be near the lifeless mess that was its mate. An hour later, the bird still sits on the wire, watching the little spot of feathers. I wonder whether anyone else passing noticed this small tragedy, and I remember a fragment of verse about swatting a mosquito: a life so small, but to itself, so dear.

Two years have gone by. I've clawed starling nests out of our martin gourds and flicker boxes every spring, but that doesn't keep the starlings from trying again and again. I've consciously tried to waste their time, to let them get as far as laying eggs before ousting them, to give native birds a chance to get established in their natural cavities. I always feel mean when I do it, because starlings didn't ask to be imported and have no idea why they're *avia non grata* on Indigo Hill. Eugene Schiefflin, an eccentric industrialist, formed a society whose charter it was to introduce to the United States every bird that Shakespeare mentioned. In the spring of 1890, the first pair of starlings nested in the eaves of the American Museum of Natural History, closely watched by ornithologists who had no idea what a Pandora's box had just been opened. Starlings have to be considered a resounding success, unless you're a native cavity-nesting bird, and then they're a disaster. There are few native birds able to outbicker a starling for a nest cavity. When starlings move in, our native birds have to move out.

Such thoughts were running through my head as I pinned up clean laundry on the line in the warm spring sunshine. I cocked an ear to the male starling sitting on the telephone wire just up the hill. He does a terrific common nighthawk imitation and an even better red-headed woodpecker, enough to make me whip my head around looking for the rarity. He barks like the neighbor's beagles, wheezes, whistles, and grunts. I love listening to his ever-changing station. It was peaceful out there, and I was getting a little modest bending exercise, saving electricity and gas, always my preferred method of drying laundry. Liam had just gone down for a rare afternoon nap, and I knew I had a couple of hours to myself. His open bed-

room window was right overhead. Suddenly Liam's sweet voice rang out. "Mommy? Mommy?" No! He couldn't be awake! My heart flopped at the possibility. And in the next instant, I realized that my little boy's voice had come not from his window to my left but from the phone wire to my right. The starling continued his litany, oblivious to his dumbfounded audience below. When I'd regained my composure, I called softly to the starling, "Mommy?" He paused, then answered, "Maaa! Maaa!" in Liam's voice again.

When I was a child, we owned an Indian hill mynah, supposedly the best talker among birds. I spent hours hunkered under his cage cover, breathing the funky cage smell, repeating simple phrases, hoping Yogi would repeat even a fragment of one. All he ever managed was a piercing whistle and some gargling burps, one of which we told people was "Hello." And now here was this wild starling speaking to me in my child's voice. "You just got your get-out-of-jail-free card, buddy!" I said to him. "You can keep your nest, and your eggs, and I'll let you raise your babies here. Any bird that calls my name in my baby's voice STAYS!"

The talking starling and his mate raised five sooty fledglings, who voiced their harsh *kwirr!* around the yard for a week or so, then left. I lowered the flicker box and, holding my nose, cleaned out the soggy nest. It had already been relined for the next brood. I like that starling, but not that much. He's still singing hopefully around the place, but he's going to have to come up with something else to amaze me if he's to get back in that flicker box. I keep glancing at the eaves, expecting a dew-spangled spider web that reads SOME STARLING! to appear. There is magic in the air this spring, magic in the starling's song.

I suppose I'll have to keep hauling starling nests out of my birdhouses, drawing a line in the sand. In their native England, starlings (and house sparrows, another European species that has wreaked havoc here) are on a precipitous decline; both are candidates for the "red list" of species of special concern. How ironic! Sometimes I wonder how long we'll keep fighting them, how long a species introduced in 1890 can or should be considered a noxious exotic. Shouldn't it have been issued a green card by now?

With exotic creatures coming in by air, land, and sea, we're moving toward a global fauna, and yet we fight and fight. To make it harder, I really like starlings. I love their rambling songs, coming from speckled flocks in the tops of maples in the crisp air of fall. I like the fact that they would think to include a mushy hot pepper or a fresh flower in their messy nests. I love the oily mix of green and purple, blue and black that runs through their spiky plumage, and the delicate touch of turquoise that paints the base of their yellow bills in spring. Find me another wild bird that can call out in my son's voice . . . And yet, when I see a starling parked in a freshly excavated flicker nest hole, my blood boils. Such is the dilemma of a bird watcher who knows a little too much about starlings.

Atoning to Box Turtles

I WALK SLOWLY. Our land is very steep, and my legs are short. I scan the ground, listening for birds in the treetops. It's April 19, and I move as if directed by an unseen hand to the winter hibernaculum of my first box turtle of spring. He sits like a jewel box in the leaves, only his head protruding, his eyes still sealed shut with the sleep of months. The sun bakes him as he basks. Behind him, a shallow burrow twice his length and just his width descends into the soft forest loam. He has spent the long winter here, barely kept from freezing solid by the insulating soil and leaves.

Feeling the vibration of my footsteps, he lifts his front foot and wipes at his left eye. Slowly it opens, and the scarlet iris, filmy with sleep, fixes on my face. *What a wake-up call*, I think. The first day out of hibernation and the first thing he sees is a human being! I help him open his right eye and gently lift him to assess his condition. He's weighty for his size, and he's come through the winter well. He's missing his right hind foot, perhaps courtesy of a raccoon. It has healed well, and the bone ends in a pearly knob he walks on. I feel the concave surface of his lower shell. This, and his red eyes, assure me of his sex; the female's eyes would be brown to red-brown, her plastron flatter. His plastron needs a scoop in it so he can balance atop the female for mating. I return him to the mouth of his burrow,

First box turtle of the season
April 25 1994
A very large male with brilliant scarlet eyes
well-marked but muddy from a winter under the earth
Wise and suspicious, he withdrew and wouldn't even
allow himself a peek at me

write some notes, and tiptoe away, elated to have been present on this turtle's first morning out.

A good number of box turtles still roam our eighty acres of woodland. Another eighty-acre parcel is kept safe by like-minded neighbors. A few years back, we bought the land that connects our two tracts. The surrounding land is a patchwork of cattle pasture, thin woodland, and agricultural fields, most of it uninhabitable for box turtles.

Predictably, our unofficial nature preserve bursts with life. May is overwhelming as the woodland rings with birdsong and glows with trillium, blue phlox, and cranesbill. Pileated woodpeckers and broad-winged hawks scold as I pass near their nests, and today a hen turkey rockets off her eggs at me like a twenty-pound feather duster. Oops! I back away and hurry out of the vicinity. Morels poke up through the leaf litter, and I move slowly along the rich slopes to gather them. The first one I find ends in a bitten-off stem. Scarcely a yard away, a female box turtle rests, a smug look on her beaked face. I will find five turtles this day, May 4, two of them already mating—a first for me. I wish them well and hope that the female finds a safe place to bury her porcelain white eggs.

As the days finally warm and gentle rains soften the ground, turtles begin to search for each other and mate. Their travels take them onto country roads and highways as ancient instincts that have served them well over life spans of fifty years or more send them out in search of their own kind. They're visible standing alert by the roadside, heads high, scanning the whizzing traffic, or perhaps in bloodied pieces where a hard wheel has ended their lives. In box turtle time, roads are quite recent, and the reptiles are helpless to overcome these barricades. Pulling in head and feet may stop a raccoon, but not a car.

My father traveled a great deal when I was a child, mostly on back roads. When he would return from a summer business trip, my sister and I would mob his car to see if he'd brought us a box turtle. As often as not, there would be a frightened captive hiding under the seat. We'd name it and feed it bananas and earthworms, then release it in the five-acre woodland behind our house. Ringed with houses and busy streets, thick with pets, lawnmowers, and other kids, it was a sorry place for wild turtles. It never occurred to us that we were dooming our temporary pets to certain death.

A box turtle that's taken from the roughly five acres it calls home and dropped in unfamiliar territory may wander aimlessly for three years or more in a vain search for familiar landmarks. In its wanderings it inevitably crosses a road or lawn, meeting cars, mowers, or curious dogs, or it finds itself back in captivity, where it will slowly waste away as a pet. It's the realization of the innocent harm I committed as a child that makes me work now to help box turtles in any way I can.

Feeling as I do about them, I look at each box turtle I find with an eye to its overall condition. I pick it up and check to see that it carries enough weight for its size, rather like hefting an orange or a grapefruit before buying it. When one comes up light (most healthy adults are just short of a pound), I look more closely to see if I can determine what's amiss.

A surprising number show signs of infection in their eyes or upper respiratory tracts. In fact, there's concern among scientists who work with them about the potential for an epidemic among box turtles, such as the bacterium *Mycoplasma agassizzi* that has ravaged desert and gopher tortoises in the Southwest. One study found that 43 percent of box turtles had been exposed to, but were not necessarily hosting, this bacterium. These results suggest that there is a *Mycoplasma* organism infecting eastern box turtles, though only one (Florida) animal has been found that was actually infected. (Because of the possibility of spreading this and other infections, scientists caution against releasing turtles of unknown origin and con-

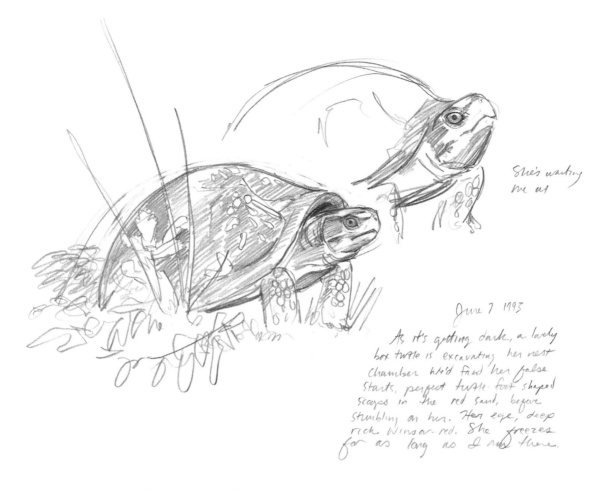

She's waiting
me at

June 7 1993

As it's getting dark, a lovely
box turtle is excavating her nest
chamber. We'd find her false
starts, perfect turtle-foot-shaped
scoops in the red sand, before
stumbling on her. Her eye, deep
rich Winsor-red. She freezes
for as long as I am there.

dition into wild populations without lengthy quarantine and evaluation before-
hand.)

I've taken turtles to veterinarians for ear infections, which can be really ex-
treme in box turtles. In the worst case I saw the ear was so swollen that a boy
brought the poor creature to his middle school classroom thinking it was a two-
headed turtle. After a veterinarian emptied the abscess surgically, I was left with a
daily regime of irrigating the wound and injecting antibiotics into the hapless turtle's hind legs for the next three weeks. It was a good test of one's love of turtles.

The first of five box turtles hatched 10/04/90 from a clutch laid 6/18/90. By Oct. 8 the other four were hatching but had not yet dug their way to the surface (~ 2½"). He tried to eat mealworms and bit his fishy-smelling eggshell several times.

egg tooth very sharp

Unabsorbed yolk sac shrinks each day. He is extremely strong and proved impossible to hold in one hand. These are all actual size. At least 8 hatched from two nests this season. I caged the nests, foiling attempts by a raccoon and a black rat snake.

The patient, a large male who had previously stalked, head up, around my studio as he looked for a way out, began to regard me with deep suspicion, especially as the hour for his morning shot drew near. He'd hide under furniture, and within three days learned to rumble away from me with his hind legs (the injection sites) tucked in.

Freed of the abscess and feeling better every day, he began to eat heartily, and I kept him over the winter, feeding him until he tipped the scales at fourteen ounces. One misty morning in spring, I drove to the school in rural Ohio where the turtle had been brought in and spoke to the boy's class about the turtle's recuperation and box turtle conservation. That afternoon, the proud student, a big, quiet boy, released his famous find in the same spot where he'd captured it a year earlier.

The boy's science teacher, who'd called me when the turtle was first brought in, told me of a hunting trip he'd taken with his father when he was a child. They had found a turtle and carved their initials into its shell before releasing it. (Not something he'd recommend to his students; it is painful and can lead to shell infections.) Returning for a little hunting in the same woodland with his now-elderly father, they found the turtle alive and well, with the initials still legible after twenty-five years.

Amazingly tough, box turtles can survive years of captivity, but not unscathed. Most long-term captives show signs of calcium depletion: sunken, ridged shells, poor color, and flaky skin. Many develop culinary tunnel vision, accepting only one type of food and refusing everything else.

Behaviorally, captivity can have strange effects. My most recent rehabilitation challenge was a box turtle that had been a family pet for eight years. Although turtles aren't particularly cuddly, this one was cuddled, stroked, chucked under the chin, and occasionally even slept with! With a daily soaking in cool water and a steady diet of canned cat food, he held up his end of the pet compact by following his owners around the house, head high, occasionally nipping at their fingers. Spoken to, he'd rear up on his front legs, a look of intense interest in his eyes. He'd tuck in his head and legs only when approached by the family cat; otherwise, he was bombproof and, by all appearances, disease-free.

As his owners learned more about box turtles, they began to realize that L.C.'s life was not all it could be, and they came to the decision to release him. Taking him back to Kentucky, where he had been found, was not an option. An Internet search led them to my modest turtle preserve, and they drove three hours on a torrentially rainy Saturday to bring him here. It was almost a month before L.C., weaned off cat food and onto fruit and night crawlers, was ready for release. I was touched by the couple's devotion to this odd little box of instinct and impulse. What they'd interpreted as affection (following and nipping) looked like hunger or some haywire dominance behavior to me. He'd sneak up on me or my toddler, staring fixedly at our hands, then begin to nip. Knowing the viselike power of a box turtle's bite, I stayed alert to his whereabouts at all times, and Phoebe took to tucking her hands into her armpits whenever L.C. trundled up to her.

In late May, Phoebe and I finally carried L.C. down to our woodland spring, where I release displaced turtles. He drank deeply, looked around at the lush undergrowth, and headed straight for us! I returned him to the spring and he started doggedly after us once again. I picked Phoebe up and turned to go. Realizing we were going to leave L.C. in the woods, Phoebe started to whimper and stretched her arms out to the animal, which was hurrying to keep us in sight. As I loped off, I reasoned that L.C. was very unlikely to bump into another human being on our preserve, and any roads he might cross are dirt and very lightly traveled. It was the best we could do for him.

Biology professor David McShaffrey of Marietta College, who has released several of his displaced or injured turtles on our farm, reassured me. "This stalking and nipping behavior is well documented in captive box turtles; they seem to be begging for food. As far as rehabilitating long-term captives, there's really no brain there to deprogram." I felt a little better and hoped L.C. would soon find a willing female turtle. I felt confident that, deprived of human contact, he'd know a night crawler, mushroom, or slug when he found one.

Sometimes rehabilitated turtles come back for a visit. As it started to turn cold one autumn, I found myself apologizing to my brother-in-law, a star chef from Baltimore, for the canned cocktail sauce I'd offered for the shrimp hors d'oeuvres he'd just prepared for us. Suddenly, I remembered having planted a few horseradish roots under our raised deck, and chef Dave and I grabbed a shovel and headed into the overgrowth in a Euell Gibbons–style search for edibles. Sorting through a jungle of spearmint, Dave said, "I don't see any horseradish, but here's a turtle!" And there, like a present, was a box turtle, with a long well-healed scar across its carapace. A loop of copper wire dangled from two drilled holes in the healed edges. I knew this fellow. A year and a half earlier, Dr. McShaffrey had brought this turtle to me for release. He'd already had it for a year, ever since its shell was crushed by a car. Sewn together with epoxy and copper wire, its shattered shell had healed slowly. And now, two and a half years after it first fell afoul of man, the same turtle sat in my horseradish patch only a hundred yards from where I'd released it. Naraht was to return sporadically each May for the next six years, staring fixedly at the front door, waiting for his breakfast of strawberries and earthworms. He'd hang around for about a week, then go off on turtle rounds, not to appear again until the next May. Even after we built an addition on our house and moved the front door, he'd find the new entrance and wait there for me to notice him. I have my doubts about McShaffrey's "no brain" hypothesis.

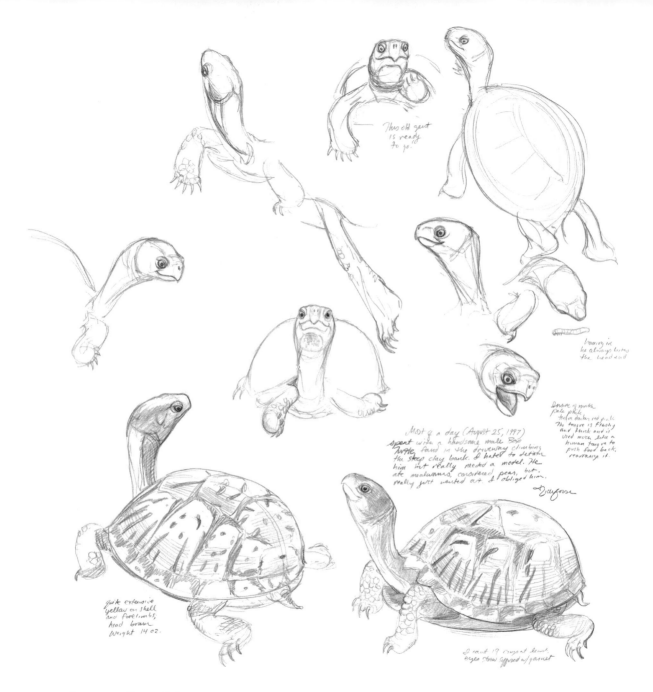

"This old gent is ready to go."

Not a day (August 25, 1997)
spent with a handsome male Box
Turtle, found in the driveway climbing
the steep clay bank. I hated to detain
him but really needed a model. He
ate mealworms, considered pear, but
really just wanted out. I obliged him.
Dreyfuss

quite extensive
yellow on shell
and forelimbs;
head brown
Weight 14 oz.

Focused as I am on helping turtles in my little corner of Ohio, it's hard for me to comprehend what has been happening to box turtles on a nationwide basis. Most of us are accustomed to seeing them along our roads and highways, but box turtles are sold for as much as $100 apiece on the European pet market. When overcollecting and habitat loss pushed the Mediterranean tortoise near extinction, European and Japanese pet collectors turned to both legal and illegal imports of American box turtles to satisfy their craving for reptiles.

Some twenty thousand box turtles per year were exported from this country in 1992 and 1993, according to the U.S. Fish and Wildlife Service. Outcry from herpetologists, conservationists, and concerned citizens led in 1994 to all North American turtles of the genus *Terrapene* being listed in the Convention on International Trade in Endangered Species of Wild Fauna and Flora (CITES). Further, the Fish and Wildlife Service set a zero quota for 1996, 1997, and 1998 for international exports from Louisiana, the only state that, in the face of public protest, persisted in shipping crateloads of box turtles abroad.

Exports in the tens of thousands, even for only a few years, may have already doomed some native box turtle populations to extinction. One study of a subspecies in Wisconsin showed that the loss of only one adult turtle per year could bring that population to extinction in the distant future. With continuing encroachment on their remaining habitat, the toll taken by vehicles, predation, disease, and pet collection may already have put many box turtle populations on the road to extirpation.

Professor William Belzer of Clarion University believes that thinning a box turtle population can lead to such low density that the animals can no longer reproduce, since their only means of detecting a potential mate is simply to run into it. They've got no call, no pheromone, no means of broadcasting their presence and thus attracting each other. Even when mates do connect and fertile eggs are laid, a legion of predators waits to devour them. In twelve years of searching for nests on our preserve, I have yet to find one before the skunks, raccoons, and crows do. The curled white eggshells litter the ground around the dug-out nests, signaling another failure. It can be hard to tell, with such long-lived animals, when a population has passed the point of no return—that is, when its replacement rate is outstripped by mortality. Although I'm out a lot looking for turtles, I've found only three juveniles in scores of encounters here—and one spent the summer with me recovering from a massive ear infection!

I have the study abstracts before me on a table, and I struggle to make sense of them, to reconcile humanity's appalling treatment of this ancient creature with common sense and prudence. For me, it all comes down to a simple issue: respect. Respect, distinct from love, for we can love a species to death. With the international pet trade, we may already have done so. Something in me chills at the thought of keeping a box turtle for a pet, of putting a creature that may be as old as my mother in a cardboard box and, for the pleasure of having it, ending its reproductive life in the wild.

I watch a video of box turtle courtship sent to me by Professor Belzer, a man possessed by box turtles and perhaps their most passionate defender. He's attempting to repatriate the forested grounds of a Pennsylvania nature center with displaced box turtles, and he videotapes their social interactions. Red eyes blazing, a male turtle approaches a female. He peers into her closed shell, then bobs his head rapidly and sways on extended legs in a fertility dance as old as carbon. It's his one-turtle campaign to keep the woodlands crawling with box turtles. I wish him, Bill Belzer, and all those who work to help box turtles the best of luck.

Baffling Phoebes

IT'S NO SECRET that I love phoebes; I'm reminded of that fact many times each day. My daughter, Phoebe, pads into the studio and asks if I have a project for her to do. I send her to her drawing table to draw me a picture of a rat snake looking at a phoebe nest. And I think about the great blessing of her presence and the small blessings now packed into a decrepit mud-and-moss nest under our deck.

When we bought our house in the winter of 1992, phoebes had nested under the deck just the summer before. Despite prayers and yearly offerings (of shelves and ledges designed just for them), no phoebes nested for the next seven years. Finally, spurning all the places we thought were suitable, a pair of phoebes arrived and built a mud nest

atop a television relay box under the deck. Four eggs hatched on May 19, 1999. They fledged all four young, who burst from the nest all at once on their seventeenth day. One of our greatest wishes had been granted.

Only three days after the young birds left, the female phoebe was relining the tired little nest for another clutch of eggs. By now, the black rat snakes that live in the cracks of our stone-and-cement patio were active, but I had taken great care to protect this precious nest. Using a combination of Plexiglas sheets, a one-by-four, a cut-up wastebasket, some old bath towels, rocks, three boards, and a whole mess of duct tape, I had constructed a wastebasket baffle for the downspout, built a roof for the nest, then stuffed all the cracks on the deck just overhead in an attempt to thwart the agile, climbing snakes. I thought I had it covered, both above and below. Three young from this second brood hatched on June 25, and they had been reduced to lumps in a five-and-a-half-foot black rat snake by the twenty-ninth. He was big enough, I surmised later, to wrap himself around the downspout and glide out and over the overturned wastebasket baffle. It was to be the phoebes' last attempt that season. They quit the place entirely in 2000. For want of a functional baffle, our phoebes were lost.

Time was when I might have removed Jake, the one-eyed rat snake, taken him to a tumbledown shed a few miles down the road, and bid him farewell. But I like him, and I like the fact that he's always working on the white-footed mice that nest in my attic and car and on the chipmunks that excavate all my planters and eat my tulip bulbs. He turns his good eye toward us as he lets my daughter stroke his scaly back, and he didn't bite my father-in-law last summer for falling out of a tippy rocking chair right on top of him. Jake belongs here as much as the phoebes do.

In the spring of 2002, a male phoebe appeared, whirling out of the woods, calling his name in an irritable, sneezy voice. He sang for more than a week and abruptly stopped singing when a female appeared on April 16. There being no

Five phoebes, about to go 6-4-02

other phoebes within earshot, he stopped advertising and started building. He shunned the shelves and ledges we'd put up all around the place and once again began to pile mud on the little plastic television relay box. Five eggs hatched, once again on May 19. A cold, wet spring kept the snakes in their lairs. On May 29, the frantic chitters of our bluebirds and soft chips of the phoebes gave unmistakable evidence of the black rat snake's emergence. I'd long since stripped away my 1999-vintage Rube Goldbergian construct (from my plastic and duct tape period). I stared numbly at the flat head of the wary snake as it watched me from the safety of the patio crack. I strode over to look up at the nest and plan a baffle system that would work this time.

I walked into the garage, looking at the piles of things that, because they just might be useful someday, had escaped the dump. My eye fell on two tempered-glass shower doors that had been a water-spotted annoyance in the bathroom but had since been recycled as part of a splendid seasonal cold frame. I put them up on either side of the downspout and used some C-clamps to hold them together in a shallow vee, edges flush to the house wall. Bricks held the base of the vee firmly. My baffle this time was four feet of sheer glass. *Try climbing that, Snakey Boy.*

Next, I took an enormous sheet of plywood to make a solid floor on the deck above and worked weather stripping putty into all the cracks around the edges. To top it off, around the ground below the nest I sprinkled powdered Spic and Span, which smells dreadful to me, and, I hoped, to the snakes.

By the fourth of June, all five young, fully feathered now, are piled atop the little mud nest. They're sixteen days old, probably no more than a day away from fledging, and I must move carefully around the nest. Phoebe nests have a tendency to explode around fledging day. I sit on the patio several yards away and sketch the young birds, using binoculars. The piercing odor of Spic and Span mingles with the powder-room scent of Japanese honeysuckle wafting from the woods. From one angle, I can see pieces of three young; from another, four. The tail of a fifth, being utterly sat upon, protrudes from beneath the pile of feathers, bills, and yellow clown lips. There'd be no way to count them unless I drew them, for to draw is to understand. I hurry, because both parents, their bills stuffed with insects, are chipping impatiently, and because I know that fledging time is near. I feel like an intruder, and yet the phoebes would be snake food but for my homemade conglomerate of glass, brick, and wood around their nest. I figure they owe me a modeling session. From a crack in the patio, a small neat head slowly protrudes and turns almost imperceptibly. He is watching. The story is never truly over.

Dancing with Tree Swallows

IT'S A COLD and rainy spring, and I worry about the tree swallows that are nesting in a box in our yard. Tree swallows are recent arrivals to southern Ohio. When we moved here in 1992, we knew of only one nest site in the county, an embayment of the Ohio River with standing dead trees, where a few pairs raised their young.

I have to confess that while I adore tree swallows, it wasn't always thus. When I first started running a trail of bluebird boxes in Connecticut in 1982, I was focused on attracting bluebirds. Any bird that gave them competition was—and I cringe to admit it—slightly annoying. Into this basket fell, of course, the house sparrow, the house wren, and the tree swallow. House sparrows, unwelcome imports from Europe with a penchant for killing incubating female bluebirds and their young, were more than annoying—they were ousted without ceremony, trapped and removed, if possible. House wrens, being native nesters, were offered another housing option and left strictly alone once they settled on a box. Tree swallows I tolerated, and I put boxes up in pairs to let both species nest, but sometimes I wished they'd leave my bluebirds alone. Once, a gang of five tree swallows killed a female bluebird and pecked her tiny nestlings, forcing me to revive them, then foster them into other bluebird nests. I was disgusted with swallows after that.

I had to move to Ohio to realize how narrow-minded I had been. Here, there were plenty of bluebirds and no tree swallows. We had to get in the car to go see them. And I missed their jingling twitter, the utter confidence with which the females sat on their nests, allowing me to lift them to count their pinkish white eggs. I missed their little turtlelike heads protruding from the box entrance and

Tree swallows about
11 days old from a yard box

their beautiful, feather-lined nests. I realized that tree swallows are every bit as deserving of nest boxes as bluebirds, every bit as beautiful, helpful, desirable. And I realized how old-fashioned my views had been, stacking and prioritizing one species over another. It took five years of deprivation, but finally there was room in my heart for tree swallows.

Five years we waited as tree swallow populations slowly built and pressed their way south from the lake country of northern Ohio. Finally, a pair occupied one of our martin gourds, only to be drowned out by horizontal rain in the ferocious flood of 1997. They returned in 1998 with another pair, and we were, at last and deliciously, rich in swallows once again. I'd never take them for granted again.

Phoebe and Liam, then six and two and a half, respectively, wake up early. I have to set an alarm to beat Liam to the dawn. But spring migration moves Bill and me to such extremes. We arose and snuck up to the tower atop our house to take in the sounds and sights of a mid-May morning. The silvery, liquid twitter of the male tree swallow drifted down from above. And suddenly, he was hovering, swinging only inches above my head. In a flash, I realized that my hair, blowing in the updraft, looked like good nesting material to him. He was talking to me, and I understood. I dashed down the stairs and rummaged in the cabinet for a package of white turkey feathers we'd bought at a craft store last year, just for the swallows.

Panting, I climbed the last flight (the tower's forty-two feet high) and raised a feather above my head. Releasing it, I watched it float across the yard. Suddenly, it was one with the swallow. He climbed, released it, and snatched it again, this time by the quill end. He swooped to the nest box and disappeared inside. Almost before I could get a second feather out and hand it to Bill, the bird was back, hovering. This time, Bill held the feather up, and the swallow, hesitating, finally snatched it from his fingers.

That was all Bill and I needed. Once again, we dashed downstairs, but this time to awaken Phoebe and Liam, bundle them into their coats and hats, and bring them, still puffy-eyed and wondering, to the top of the tower. We set each atop a chair and gave each a feather. Liam released his, just to watch it float down, but Phoebe held hers up. The two children huddled together, watching the feather. Up

A tree swallow takes a goose
feather to his box

swooped the swallow, hovering less than a foot from their faces. His bill snapped as he took the feather from Phoebe's fingers. Liam gave a baby yell of triumph, then we all hooted with laughter. "Buwd! It's a buwd!" he shouted.

We gave that swallow a dozen or more feathers, learning to hold them by their fluffy tips and let him grab them by the quill. If we forgot, he'd release them in flight and maneuver around to hold them by the quill end, just as an osprey adjusts a newly caught fish to be carried head forward for streamlining.

Finally, when the swallow and our arms tired, we trooped down the stairs and out to the nest box to see how the female swallow had arranged her feathery gifts. Quills down, she'd inserted them into the grassy nest lining beneath her six eggs. Their tips curved over the nest cup, a dome of white feathers, insulating and protecting the eggs from the chilly morning air. The children looked in wonder. Liam murmured, "Eggs. In a nest. Buwd nest." As we closed the box and started back toward the house, Bill began to fret that he'd be late for his staff meeting.

"It doesn't get any better than this, honey," I soothed. "If you can't do things like this with your family, what's all that hard work for?"

A recent study in New York State showed that tree swallow nest success could be predicted in large part by the number of feathers in each nest. Fewer feathers mean a less-insulated nest, more parasites, perhaps less-experienced parents, and all of this translates into a lower number of fledglings in sparsely feathered nests. The more feathers lining a nest, the greater number of young might be expected to fledge from it. I had to smile as I caught myself, the former tree swallow intolerant, hoping we'd fledge all six.

Big Nature

I LIKE INSECTS. I'll let a praying mantis light foot over my arm, catch a squishy black field cricket with my hand, sort mealworms by the thousands. But this is a year to try even my soul. Here in southern Ohio, we're deep into the much-ballyhooed hatch of Brood V of the seventeen-year periodic cicada. I've looked forward to living through a hatch again since the first and only one I experienced, as a first-grader in Virginia. (I missed the second cycle. I think I was contra dancing in New England.) I have dim childhood memories of hanging the cicadas' dried brown nymphal cases all over my shirt and grossing out my friends, but that's about it.

I was showing some biology students around our sanctuary the morning the cicadas first started emerging. I whooped and snatched the first one I saw, all bronzy black with red eyes and big orange-veined cellophane wings. Partway into my explanation about the cicada's bizarre life cycle, the students began murmuring and pointing around. They were . . . *everywhere*!

Over the next few days, the cicadas would emerge by the tens of thousands, even the millions, coating the old apple and pear trees with cast skins. The pale white soft-bodied adults struggled out of the split cases, their exoskeletons slowly darkening and hardening, shivering their strong thoracic muscles with a muted

rattle. Otherwise, they were eerily silent. A week later, we awoke to a low hum, as of a distant jet engine just warming up. It was an expectant sound, slightly ominous to my ears. *Is that all they do?* I wondered.

In the next three days, a skirling, stuttering buzz overlaid the hum, and it slowly swelled and grew. Sixteen days after the first cicadas emerged, I had to admit that the din was frightening. I didn't go out in the heat of the day. The swelling roar from the surrounding forest hurt my ears. Even inside the house I was irritable. It's the same feeling I get when a football game blares from a television for too long (say, three hours too long). I took to walking outside at dusk, when the cicadas all fell mercifully silent.

None of this was lost on the birds, and the cicada hatch, along with the fair weather, made for a boom year in nesting. After my awe on seeing their numbers had subsided, my first thought about the cicadas was *Wonder what eats them?* Anything that hatches out in such abundance must be good to eat, otherwise why have a saturation strategy? A cedar waxwing was the first bird we saw sampling the bounty, astonishing us by bashing, then swallowing an adult cicada whole, wings and all. Wow. I guess a wide gape that can handle a bing cherry is preadapted for a whole periodic cicada.

The bluebirds in our yard, habitual mealworm junkies, stopped begging for handouts, and the deck was littered with cicada thoraces and wings—the bluebirds prefer the abdomens à la carte. Cicada carcasses turned up in the bluebird boxes, evidence that the adults were at least trying to feed them to their young. Comparing notes with James R. Hill III, founder of the Purple Martin Conservation Association, I learned that adult martins love the slightly larger "dog day" cicadas, but are largely unsuccessful in stuffing them into their nestlings. Perhaps the same holds true of the periodic cicadas. Our tree swallows ignored them but fledged a

healthy brood nonetheless. Our phoebes, even the four fledglings from the first brood, grew adept at bashing the cicadas' abdomens free of their thoraces, then swallowing them, bluebird style. We watched an eastern kingbird in hot pursuit of a flying cicada, and a flicker swooped overhead with one jutting from its bill. A friend reported seeing indigo buntings, house sparrows, and cardinals taking them. Brown thrashers hopped about on the lawn like robins, lazily spearing cicadas. It must have been nice for them to not have to wonder where to find their next meal.

Perhaps the most obvious benefit accrued to our wild turkeys. Each summer,

the dusky hens lead their ever-shrinking broods through our meadows and lawn. Each hen starts out with perhaps a dozen small poults, and by late July perhaps three or four remain to tag along behind her. Sometimes two hens will team up, gather their young into a crèche, and share the burden of keeping track of them. This summer was different. Three hens joined forces, perhaps of necessity, with an enormous crèche of fat, cicada-fed poults. It was impossible to count them accurately, as they darted in and out of the tall vegetation, but from our high deck I could get a pretty good idea that there was a whole mess o' turkeys out there.

It wasn't until I was out picking black raspberries that I saw the whole flock. Every year, I ruin a good T-shirt when I stumble on the ripe fruit and heedlessly turn my shirtfront into a purple-stained picking pouch. This day, the turkeys and I had the same idea, but they had the sense to eat the berries as they picked them. Suddenly, a low *putt* from one of the hens sent the entire brood into orbit. Three launches sent dozens of poults hurtling toward the woods as I counted frantically. Whipping out my notebook, I made a sketch of the flock as I had just seen it, then counted my dots: forty-five. I had always assumed that predation whittled down the poults' ranks, and it doubtless does; this summer, the predators were feasting on cicadas rather than turkeys. It's high-quality forage. Foxes, coyotes, raccoons, skunks, and opossums all took advantage, and I even saw a woodchuck scavenging the insects from the blacktop!

I imagine the list of birds that spent the first part of the summer eating cicadas. Scarlet and summer tanagers, with their strong, heavy bills, are likely candidates, as are orioles, blackbirds, and meadowlarks. Woodpeckers of all kinds. Jays, most certainly, crows, and kestrels. By night, screech-owls would doubtless share them with barred owls. Whip-poor-wills and nighthawks might snag any that flew toward dusk or dawn. I wonder if the smaller chickadees, titmice, and nuthatches learned to stash them and carve them up, like tiny turkeys. None of these birds, save the long-lived crows and raptors, could have been around for the last hatch. We were all winging it, drinking in the experience in our own way.

I have to admit that by the time the cicadas finally began to die in late June, I was ready for the funeral. In fact, a surveillance camera would have repeatedly captured me outside, shaking my fists, shouting, "Hurry up and die already, you little creeps!" before darting toward the house. As if mocking me, flying cicadas made beelines for my head and back whenever I ventured out. As many as five or six would land on me at once and, adding insult to psychic injury, shriek *weeoo weeoo weeoo* as I tried to dislodge them. Living amidst their constant, deafening screeching, watching them swarm over my beloved Japanese maples, fruit trees, birches, weeping willow, buddleia, and even my potted bonsais, mercilessly top-pruning them all with their razor-sharp ovipositors, was too much. Every tree on the woodland's edge hung with brown, dead branchlets severed by the egg-laying cicadas' probes, each one bursting with white cicada eggs. As these branches fell to the ground, the nymphs hatched out and burrowed into the soil for their seventeen-year adolescence, sucking juices from tree roots, making secret tunnels yards below our unwitting feet. The trees would survive the pruning, though my bonsais will bear the scars for the rest of their days. I've decided that they add character to the old maples, trees I've tended since I left college.

Much as the constant din and the feeling of being an unwilling insect aircraft carrier wore on my nerves, I still loved the Brood V hatch experience, the way I love big surf, thunderstorms, and oversized rat snakes. They're all reminders that nature is bigger, far bigger, and more powerful than we usually care to admit. Just as the hatch was starting, I stood in line at my favorite garden center behind a young man who was buying two gallons of a deadly liquid insecticide. He was hoping to stop the cicada hatch, to save his trees from what he was sure would be the death of them. The nursery manager rang up the sale, and his eyes met mine as the young man handed over his money. We shook our heads and smiled. I went home to watch the celebration.

Early
Goldenrod
Solidago
juncea

Mist flower
Eupatorium coelestinum
(I call this wild
ageratum).

SUMMER

Tall Ironweed
Vernonia altissima
(New York has long thread like tips or bracts)

Butterfly Weed
Asclepias tuberosa

Paradise Lost

Big, Medium, and Tiny Fergus fresh from the farm pond

AS I WRITE, there is a large pickle jar, with a huge bullfrog in it, sitting by the typewriter. His gold-flecked eye stares expressionlessly; his throat pulses gently. It is marbled with cream and olive, the softest of skins. His sturdy arms are extended, four delicate fingers pigeoned in, holding his head just above the water in the bottom of the jar. Tympanic membranes the size of a roofing nail head proclaim him a male. From snout to rump, he's nearly five inches long; in full leap, he'd stretch another five. He's a big frog.

It's hard to believe that only a year and four days ago, he first hauled himself out of the water and onto a new red lily leaf in my little backyard water garden here in southeastern Ohio.

JUNE 1, 1994: A pickle jar aswarm with seven fat bullfrog tadpoles arrives. Friends have brought them from their farm pond to enliven the 200-gallon pondlet Bill dug for me on the first of May. I watch them squiggle, judging all to be in their second year of tadhood. (Bullfrogs require two seasons as tadpoles; the transformation comes in their second summer of life.) I tip them into the pond, and they disappear in its olive depths.

JUNE 17: The tadpoles are the size of apricots, but still no legs show.

JULY 14: I return from a trip to South Africa to find them sporting big hind legs and the buds of front legs! It won't be long now.

JULY 17: Their tails are starting to shrink away, and all four legs now dangle in the water. Their eyes are getting bulbous, and they look distinctly froggy.

JULY 26: A new bullfroglet sits proudly on a red lily leaf. He's so much larger than the others, all still tadpoles, that I name him Big Fergus. Fergus seems such a fine name for a frog that I name the rest Medium, Little, and Tiny Fergus. Dumb, but effective.

AUGUST 1: I resolve to hand-tame the frogs. Placing mealworms on a flat rock in Big Fergus's sightline, I wait, froglike, hunkered at poolside. He swims over and engulfs them, starting his career as a professional freeloader.

AUGUST 4: I enjoy daily feedings with Big Fergus. Despite my efforts, the other froglets, which have since transformed, never learn to connect me with delicious mealworms, or are naturally too shy to take advantage of the offering. Big Fergus is clearly Überfrog.

By summer's end, I can smoothly slide my palm under Big Fergus and hold him up to admire his froggy grin. He's quite a creature, swimming up expectantly whenever I appear, spurning the attentions of strangers. No dunderhead, he. I am fond of him, shameless about making a pet of him, though I know his to be cupboard love, nothing more.

October comes, and I have to clean my little ecosystem, for although the water is clear, great swirling clouds of sediment rise when the koi snuffle along its bottom. On the twelfth, I clean the pool, netting all the fish and their myriad offspring and catching four frogs, all that made it of the seven tadpoles. I put them in a big plastic tub and set about draining and scrubbing. Looking over to check, I see Big Fergus, his arms hanging over the tub edge. He gathers his hind legs onto the rim and launches a glorious arc, three feet through the cool fall air and *splat!* into the now-empty pool that once was his refuge. That had to hurt.

I catch him and return him to the tub, putting a garbage can lid on it to contain him. I hear him thunking against it the whole time I labor in the pool. Returned at last to the sparkling clean pond, he hides for a whole week, sulking, I imagine.

By the second of November, the fish are motionless on pond bottom, and the frogs are no longer heard. A stillness settles over the pool. Ice creeps over its surface, and I keep the pump running so the water will stay at least partly open. Snow drifts over the ice, making an igloo out of the fountain, and I hear only a trickle beneath. I wonder how the frogs are faring and marvel at the great evolutionary distance between us, pet or no: Fergus stays under that snow and ice, on the pond's bottom, for months at a time, stilled like a run-down clock, but he is alive. I stick my hand in the water to experience his parallel world. Pain shoots up my arm like fire before three seconds are up, and I have to run inside and turn on the hot water tap to warm it. I hope he's all right down there.

Winter slithers by, finally sighs, and gives over to spring. Woodcocks *peent* and whirl over the meadow. Finally comes The Day: March 18, clear, in the sixties, and warm enough for me to don shorts and wade into the pond. Silt swirls again. I decide to clean it of winter's ooze and make a mental note to forget the fall cleaning next year. All four frogs have made it through; I feel them against my toes in the muck. I repeat the exercise with the tub, forget to lid it, only to have Big Fergus splat into the empty pond at my feet once more. Has he grown over the winter? He looks enormous, but he's all dark olive drab, the color of wet bark, without the bright green head of summer. It will be the tenth of May before he feels up to eating his mealworms, and then we continue the daily feedings as before. I can almost see him grow.

MAY 16, 1995: Fergus voices his first tentative mating call, *rumm rumm rumm*, waking us at dawn. I wonder whether it's a good idea to have a big male bullfrog in residence right under the bedroom windows. Luckily, he's too young to be in full voice and gives it up after a few days.

Big seems to be more and more voracious. Today, June 13, he mistakes my pinky finger for a mealworm and tries valiantly to stuff it down his great throat with his four-fingered hands. I feel the viselike serrated edges of his jaws and am glad to pull my finger out of his mouth, flipping him into the pond with a laugh. Still, there was something chilling about his strength; I remember the same shiver in my bones when a praying mantis I was feeding grabbed me instead of the grasshopper I offered her. She bent her triangular head and began to gnaw on my finger, and I got a flash of what it must be like to be prey.

JUNE 22: I look down from the bedroom window to see Fergus gaily bow-tied by the wings of a great spangled fritillary as it disappears down his throat. More and more, he sits facing the sweet William, which is covered with the orange butterflies, launching himself up into it to snag them. It doesn't seem to make any

difference how many mealworms I give him; he's insatiable, seeming to turn each meal into a half-inch of girth and length. The tall yellow coreopsis, bigger than a bushel basket and covered with buds, bursts into bloom at poolside, and the fritillaries swarm onto it, too. Little by little, the side of the coreopsis that faces the pond is denuded as Big hurls himself into it, amputating the flowers as he snaps shut on swallowtails and fritillaries, pearl crescents and sulfurs. This is not good; this is not what I'd envisioned. I have planted a death garden for butterflies.

A July morning, and I am cleaning the pond filter when I notice a tiny white-tipped hummingbird tail feather afloat on the surface of the pool. Then another, and another, until I retrieve all ten. The shafts are bent in the same place, just above their tips, so I know the feathers were pulled out with force and all at one time. I glare at Fergus, who regards me impassionately and swims closer with an easy flex of his great webs. When he's hungry, his sides sink in and his back ridges stand up like a bridge superstructure. But this morning, his sides are full and round. There's a young ruby-throated hummingbird in there, and I don't need X-ray spectacles to know it.

I wonder at the chances of Fergus's catching another hummingbird. Maybe it was a fluke, a chance snag, never to be repeated. The butterflies are bad enough, but I can't have him eating the hummingbirds we feed and encourage with bee balm and trumpet vine, fuchsia and coralbells. Only a week later I am shocked to find yet another set of tail feathers floating. A frog dropping floats beside them. I retrieve it and find it packed with feathers. They dry in the sun, glinting iridescent green: Another hummingbird has gone to fuel Fergus's habit. My blood chills. I realize that Fergus's constant station just beneath the pink water lily blossoms has little to do with froggy aesthetics. He's catching the hummingbirds as they come in to feed. What have I done?

August 2: I've been attempting to swamp Fergus with food, as if that were possible. He turns it all into brawn. I lean down to pick up a huge grasshopper, his favorite fare of late, and look for Fergus under his shady rock ledge, where he retreats when the sun grows hot. He is there, and there is something sticking out of his mouth. Feathers. With a strangled cry, I move over and slip my hand up under him to get a closer look. He's having none of it and dives deeply beneath the silent lily pads. Soon he pops up, and I unceremoniously grab his fat hind legs with one hand, the bird's tail with the other. I work it back up out of his gullet, far enough to see that it's a chipping sparrow and quite dead. Furious, I race up the basement stairs, frog in fist, giving Fergus his first and last tour of the house. I grab my camera to fire off a couple of shots of the culprit, caught. Still in my grip, he gulps once, and the sparrow's tail and limp foot vanish. His sides are very round now. I plop him in a pickle jar, the same one he arrived in as a tadpole, and plan his future.

The pond seemed so right with a bullfrog as its animus. He might have been cast of bronze for his color and sheen but for his glorious gold-flecked eyes. I was very fond of him and proud of myself for hand-taming him. I even staged a couple of snapshots of myself kissing him on his hard lips, the princess and her prince. Now I could throttle him. I'm confused. I'll stand at the kitchen window, agog and aglow as a sharp-shinned hawk snags a goldfinch from the feeder, and applaud its prowess even as I feel a twinge of remorse for the finch. Why am I so furious at Fergus? Why do I feel so betrayed? Fergus is just being a frog, as the sharp-shin is being a hawk. Bullfrogs, I have come to learn, eat birds. Bullfrogs, in fact, eat anything they can cram in their mouths. They live by simple rules. If it moves and you can swallow it, eat it.

I think the root of my horror is this: I thought I had control over my little ecosystem. I change the filter to keep the water clear, feed the fish sparingly, plant lots of underwater and floating vegetation for cover and breeding, keep the pump running to boost the oxygen content of the water. I conduct water changes to refresh the pond when it's hot and muggy, net out the baby shubunkin goldfish to sell or give away, divide the plants when they threaten to choke the water. I brought in bullfrogs because they seemed a natural part of this aquatic world. I figured they'd snag crickets and grasshoppers that sun on the rocks, and they did. But Fergus had plans of his own. Bullfrogs will be bullfrogs. They're not top-of-the-line predators, but in my little biosphere, they're darn close.

The sharp-shin flying free and the bullfrog in my palm are not so very different, and I can't blame either for finding its natural prey. It is I who have set up this microcosm where birds flock to feeders and sparrows bathe at the water's edge next to shady ledges, where hummingbirds buzz and hover over scented lilies, where death waits just beneath the surface. Our pond is the only water for perhaps a quarter-mile around, and in a dry summer, as all summers here seem to be, it's mobbed with birds delighted to find a splashing fountain on withered old Scott's Ridge.

Fergus is a spider with a four-by-six-foot web. He's got to go.

I make a couple of sketches of him as he sits and pulsates. I will miss him, but I won't miss the floating tail feathers or the sinking feeling I've been getting whenever a bird drinks at water's edge. I call our neighbors and ask permission to release a large bullfrog into their farm pond, explaining a little sheepishly what has happened. It won't be the first time our neighbors have scratched their heads over me, nor the last. They graciously consent.

Fergus and I trek over an alfalfa field down to the pond, I puffing, he sloshing in his jar. It seems barren, devoid of emergent vegetation. A classic farm pond, it's just a hole in the ground with some water in it and a neatly weed-whacked edge. Still, I see some pondweed just below the surface and lots of insects on the water, and I figure Fergus can make it here. His chances of snagging birds will be greatly diluted by many more square yards of shoreline and fewer places to lurk unseen.

I tip the jar and Fergus hesitates. I nudge him out into the water and he just sits. This does not compute in his tiny brain; this is not his home. *Come on, Ferg, I* coax. *Just swim away and I'll be done with you.* In the end, I have to toss him into deeper water and he dives slowly, then pops up in the featureless pond, as plain as a pimple on a cover girl. Oh, dear. Now, what have I done? This frog knows nothing about predators. What's the opposite of a Midas touch, I wonder, because I have it. I caused the demise of who knows how many hummingbirds and sparrows and fritillaries, and now I'm screwing up this frog's future. He's too far out to retrieve, and I reluctantly turn for home. Good night, sweet prince.

Back home, the pond seems quiet and sad without its thrumming tyrant. The three smaller frogs surface rarely; they're hardly big enough to swallow a cricket, much less a bird. *It was a grand run, Fergus,* I muse, *you have to hand me that. You grew more in a year than most frogs do in their lives. We had some fun, then you had to go and spoil it.* I'm humbled by it all, hit by the realization that nature will assert itself whatever we wish or plan. You put up a feeder, you get a sharp-shin strafing it; you dig a pond and put tadpoles in it, name one and hand-tame him, and he thanks you by

turning hummingbirds into frog muscle. Still, I wish him the best and hope he makes it, a not-so-big frog in a very large pond.

The next afternoon, I drive slowly by Fergus's new home, searching the water's edge for his familiar shape. There is a great blue heron standing on the shore, looking out over the smooth water.

POSTSCRIPT: FERGUS'S LEAP FROM GRACE

It's been eleven years since Fergus was banished. That same October, when the migrating warblers paused to drink and bathe at the pool, Medium Fergus took it upon himself to off a yellow-rumped warbler. Out came the net and into a cooler went Medium, Little, and Tiny Fergus. A frogfest. They were taken to a park with a cattail-choked pond, where I'm sure they're toasting yet with jugs o' rum.

Spring 1996 was frogless until a couple of pairs of American toads decided to trill and spin their gooey strings of eggs around the pond. The koi and goldfish ate all but a few of the tadpoles. That won't stop the toads, who never seem to check to see what became of their eggs but just lay more.

Nineteen-ninety-six was a wet year, and frogs were on the move. To my great delight, two green frogs, smaller, less bird-lethal cousins of the bullfrog, moved in and made the pond their new home. I thrilled to the off-tune banjo twang and the low growls of the little greens, and their funny, froggy *YIKES!* when I'd walk by the pond.

Come spring of 1997, warm days would find the two green frogs sitting on rock ledges around the pond. Had I waited, they'd have come; there was no need to import bullfrogs. They look fine sitting there or floating on the surface, and I've grown fond of them. But I'm not going to feed them or tame them; it's enough that they're here. Lesson learned.

There are a lot of water gardens in America, and I'd bet that many of them have a resident bullfrog or two. The tadpoles are even sold by the big water garden supply houses, touted as part of the "cleaning crew," eating algae alongside scavenging snails. I don't know how many water gardeners attach any significance to a few tail feathers floating on their ponds; fewer still probably dry and dissect frog droppings or happen to catch a bullfrog red-handed, stuffing a bird down its gullet. But it might behoove all of us to watch for signs of frog predation and to think twice before introducing this voracious predator to our miniature Edens.

Once Bitten

WE LIVE OUT OF TOWN, eighteen miles to be exact, and we have to climb our forty-two-foot bird watching tower to see any other houses. We like it that way, mostly. It cuts down on door-to-door solicitors (no thin mints or raffle tickets, thanks) and feuds with neighbors (so far, none). It lets us be as loud or as quiet as we want, lets us wander around wearing strange, mismatched outfits, do odd things at odd hours. I dump my compost in a pit for the coons and crows to pick over, and nobody complains. I was returning from this task, drippy compost container in hand, practicing a new song for our band's gig the next evening, "Chain of Fools," made popular by Aretha Franklin, among others, in the tough but not impossible key of C. My bandleader husband thought C was necessary for an authentic Motown sound. I wasn't quite getting it to my satisfaction. If Aretha is the Queen of Soul, I am her humble handmaiden. Wailing, squealing, cracking, I moseyed across the lawn. And from the adjoining woodland came an answer, ringing out through the midafternoon sunshine. *Yip, yip, yip, arooooooooo!* Three coyotes raised the hair on the back of my neck with their vocal stylings. I decided to bring it down to B flat.

These are the kind of neighbors I most want. I like being able to run into town and see the two-legged kind, then come back out to my wild fortress. It's only oc-

The copperhead that got me
It was very calm, and not the l[...]
bit sorry. Probably only about 1½[...]

casionally inconvenient or dangerous to be sequestered like this. Losing a car key, for example: Well, you just don't go anywhere until you find that key. Ditto for jumping a dead battery. If you can't scare up any neighbors within a mile or two, you're out of luck. You make sure your battery and tires are up to scratch. You become unusually devoted to your four-wheel-drive vehicle; whether you look stylish driving matters not when you've got ten miles of icy hills and hairpin curves to negotiate on a February morning.

You're your own ambulance when you live this far out. Weeding the ancient lavender shrubs that line my garage one July morning, I felt two suspicious pin-pricks on my left index finger. They were quick and hot, and I instinctively stuck my finger in my mouth and started sucking on it for all I was worth. When I took it out to look, the whole finger was swollen, already purple. The copperhead I had disturbed from a summer morning's reverie looked blankly back at me from its lair beneath the twisted lavender stems. Of course, I was alone; Bill had taken a rare golf date. The nearest neighbors did not answer their phone. No time to lose. I pulled my outdated reptile guide from the shelf and looked up First Aid for Snakebites. Sucking and spitting, good. I had done that. Elevate the affected member. I could do that. Get to a hospital. All right.

I climbed in the car and started the twenty-five-minute drive to town, my still-swelling finger sticking merrily up above the wheel. Living as we do in the land of the Rural One-Finger Wave, everyone I passed on the way in returned my inadvertent greeting. *Hi. Hi there. How ya doin'?* After what seemed like hours, I arrived at the "rapid-care" facility in town we irreverently refer to as "Doc in a Box" to be greeted by a shocked look from the receptionist. She turned me away, saying, "We don't deal with snakebites. You'll have to go to the emergency room." *Oh, fine. I'll just drive on. It's a nice day, and this is kind of fun. Don't mind my big, purple, sausage-sized finger . . .*

In the end, the emergency room doctors (who all crowded around for a respectful look at me) elected to do nothing, since antivenin is not something to be dispensed lightly, thanks to the possibility of an allergic reaction that could be worse than the snakebite. Since I was judged at risk for another snakebite, which, if it connected with a fleshy bit, would likely be worse than this one on my bony knuckle, they just watched me for a couple of hours as I relaxed on a gurney with my finger in the air. In retrospect, I'm glad I've been bitten and gotten off so lightly. Now I weed the lavender before the snakes stir in the spring, and I never stick my hands where I can't see.

Last season, I captured and relocated four adult copperheads from our yard; they like to bask on the warm sidewalk, where my children ride their trikes and tractors. I pinned them with a stick, picked them up by their tails, put them in a bucket, and drove them two miles down the road. Most people think I'm crazy to let them live. I do it because they belong here, and I do it to thank the three-footer, sunning in the garage doorway, that allowed my little daughter to back her bicycle over it before she noticed it. Run over by training wheels, the copperhead simply looked at her as she froze in horror. I picked Phoebe up, carried her away, caught the placid snake, and relocated it. *Thank you, Snake. Live long and well. Just live somewhere else.*

Stopping to Help

WHEN WE FIRST MOVED to southern Ohio in 1992, I saw things I couldn't identify: plants, trees, lawn ornaments, that kind of thing. I'd spent a lot of time along the eastern seaboard, and there were cultural differences for which I came unprepared. After making several trips to the grocery store in town, I was stumped by some things I'd seen on the asphalt. They looked kind of like moose droppings from a moose that had been eating an awful lot of roughage. Even if we'd been in moose country, a grocery store parking lot was an unlikely latrine. I told Bill, "I'm seeing some kind of dropping in the Kroger parking lot, and I can't figure out what's leaving it." I described the mystery wads to Bill, who frowned for a moment, then started to laugh.

"Those, my dear, are chaws."

I looked back at him blankly. "Chaws?"

"Chewing tobacco. Red Man, Mail Pouch. The guys don't want to have to spit in the store, so they dump their chaws in the parking lot as they're getting out of their cars."

Ah. Chaws. *Vive la différence.*

I'm now expert at stepping over chaws in parking lots, and I no longer give them even a second glance. Tonight, when I take Phoebe into town for her swimming lesson, I am sitting at a stoplight on Putnam Street. I glance at a little gray-brown clod in the middle of the brick street and realize in a split second that it is not a chaw; it is a baby mourning dove, much too young to be out of the nest. I throw the car into park and leap out, chasing the fluttering baby in a circle around my car. I'm surprised what a good race the little thing gives me. It's barely bigger than a house sparrow, but it trundles along just ahead of me, flapping weakly. By

the time I catch it and leap back into the car, the light has turned green. An elderly couple waiting at the cross-street light shares a laugh at my expense. The indignity is well worth it. I turn the corner, panting, and park, stuffing the bird into a small tissue box for the moment. It's much too young to have fledged; it's only about four inches long and newly feathered, still covered with pinfeathers on its crown. It's probably only about twelve days old. I walk a few yards to the first crab apple

Doves in a crabapple aside the Betsey Mills Club—one of these babies was in the middle of Putnam Street till I put it back

tree on the block, look up, and immediately spy a female mourning dove feeding a baby identical to this one in a flimsy twig and straw nest about twenty feet overhead. That sure was easy.

The tree would be no trick at all to climb. But the more I look at it, the more I realize that the branches I would have to stand on in order to reach the nest are about the thickness of a broom handle. The nest itself is on a whip-thin longitudinal branch, and I risk dislodging the whole thing just trying to haul myself up to it. That would be good: Dump the second baby and then have two to care for. Worse than that, I don't know how strong crab apple wood is, and I don't relish the thought of plunging to the ground and breaking a limb for the sake of a homely little dove. I need a fifteen-foot stepladder. At seven on a Wednesday evening.

I walk into the open doors of the Betsey Mills Club, a kind of combination young ladies' residence-gymnasium-restaurant-preschool, where my little son is enrolled for the fall. It's just the kind of portmantcau placc that small towns like Marietta have. It's after dinnertime, and I have little hope that anyone will be around to help me. The receptionist uses a walkie-talkie to contact Jim, the maintenance man. He answers after four tries. He's a lanky, friendly man who sizes up the situation, disappears, and returns with the loveliest yellow fifteen-foot stepladder I've ever seen. He sets it up under the crab apple; I skitter up and am suddenly looking Mama MoDo right in the eye. "Sorry, sweetie. You'll have to leave for a minute." She clatters off with a great flourish, and I place the errant chick right beside its warm little sibling. I wait to see that it settles down, skitter back down the ladder, shake Jim's hand, thank him, and am on my way. He seems genuinely touched by the scene. Elapsed time for the entire rescue: twelve minutes. Had I not been able to find the nest or get a ladder up to it, I'd have been saddled with raising that bird for the next month. I've raised two mourning doves, and they're a joy, but I'd so much rather it grow up as it was meant to, with other doves.

The next night, I take Phoebe into town for her last swimming lesson, and we swing by the mourning dove nest tree for a look. Mother dove is there, and there are two sweet round heads bobbing beside her. One is looking right at us. I wonder if it is the baby I saved. What a lovely feeling to know that it's home, and not just a sad little mat of feathers on the bricks of Putnam Street. A nest check two days later reveals two heads, and two days after that the nest is vacant. I smile broadly at the flimsy nest in the crab apple tree, a happy ending.

In late July, baby season to wildlife rescuers, I find it hard to go anywhere without seeing a young bird or other creature that needs a little help. I don't seek them out; rather, they present themselves to me. I have a friend who always marvels at the amazing things I see and find and sometimes wind up raising.

On my way to town the next week, I spot a lovely male rufous-sided towhee hit on a dangerous curve and laboriously turn the car around to collect it. I'm glad I did, because the poor soul is still gasping when I pick him up. Better he die in loving hands than under a wheel. I reflect on the strange bird coincidences that seem to follow me this summer, even more than usual. And know that it's simply because I am looking, and seeing, and present for these things that happen everywhere, all the time.

I stop at a little farm market where I love to pick over local corn, melons, peaches, and other things the raccoons on our land won't allow me to grow. No chaws in the parking lot this time, but I notice a silver-spotted skipper butterfly struggling between a row of strawberry jam jars and the plate-glass window of the market. I make a beeline to the spot where it's trapped and gently pinch its wings together along the leading edge to keep it from struggling all the scales off them. I walk outside and free it, rejoicing in its bounding, erratic flight as it finds a weedy

Spotted Joe-Pye Weed
Eupatorium
maculatum

Sept 8 2005

strip along the road where it can rest. I wonder how long the butterfly had been fluttering there, how many people had walked by without giving it a glance. Two men leaning against a box of melons give me a long look as I come back in the door, smiling a secret smile.

5-06-93
big brilliant ♀ (dark red eyes) ^brown
on trail to spring (1-expane)
They never seem particularly pleased
to see us - they freeze in mid-stride
(not hard for a turtle) and wait for us to
go away. She has fancy polkadot-yellow
legs and jaguar paws on her back-
creamy throat, pulsing hyoid when she
takes a big breath

There was a movie I loved with all my childish heart: *Thomasina*. The title character was a cat that died and, with the help of a woman thought to be a witch by the townspeople, returned to tell stories of its nine lives. I never tired of the movie, for I identified completely with the unusual woman who lived deep in the woods, taking in hurt animals and healing them with patience and love. In my heart, I knew I would be a strange woman just like her someday. When I see a box turtle trying to cross a road, I pull over and carry it where it wants to go. The last person who had to stop her car and wait until I was out of her way—a matter of perhaps thirty seconds—swore and nearly hit me as she whipped past. That's all right. To her, it's only a turtle, and I'm a fool. I don't mind scrambling around in public after baby birds and trapped butterflies. I don't mind the strange looks and smirks that inevitably follow such activities. I can't walk by creatures in need. And I get to take home the greatest treasure of all: a warm glow, knowing that one more turtle will lay her eggs; one more dove, one more skipper will fly because I stopped to help.

Summer Pleasures

I DON'T KNOW who or what weather system to thank, but we've had weeks of flawless summer days, the sky an arc of blue, smiling little cumulus clouds floating over. It's never too hot and delightfully cool at night, walking weather, sleeping weather. This being southern Ohio, I know it won't last, so I take advantage of it while it's here. Phoebe is five now, and we talk as we walk out to the meadow or the long gravel driveway. A little elm tree stands, covered with wisteria, the pernicious legacy of the old farmstead that once graced the hill east of our house. The four main branches of the elm reach up as if in supplication, smothering in vines. "Why does that tree look like a monster's hand?" Phoebe asks me.

"Because it's covered with wisteria vine, and it makes the tree look like a monster's claw," I answer.

"No wonder they call it mysterious vine," she muses, and I suppress a hoot of laughter and file wisteria's new name away in my Phoebe file.

We make a couple of trips out to the vegetable garden, one in the early morning and one in the late afternoon to harvest our supper. So far, the raccoons have taken every tomato as it ripens. I am on my hands and knees, assessing the damage when Phoebe exclaims, "Mommy! More of your viruses are blooming!" I look up, and she's standing next to a gladiolus that's taller than she is. I wonder how many times I laughed every day before Phoebe arrived, how I did without her.

It's baby season. Baby birds are everywhere, peeping and squirking in the big pussy willow, the sumac, the raspberry tangles. Baby scarlet tanagers, all olive, voice a plaintive *jerwert* from the top of an ash as their flame-colored father bustles around between them. Baby Baltimore orioles, who, like cardinals, vocalize every waking moment, constantly remind their parents that they're here and they're *hungry*! A fledgling

A baby indigo snugged up against a Va. pine trunk Just fledged - Dad is the bald feeder visitor. 7/03/01 Whipple home

prairie warbler follows a young oriole to my recirculating birdbath for its first dip.

The nervous *spit* calls of our pair of indigo buntings heralds the explosion of their nest, four bits of coffee brown, tailless shrapnel scattered around the site. Phoebe and I admire one tiny fledgling clinging in a Virginia pine. It still wears yellow clown lips, and it looks like something you'd find bagged in cellophane in the craft aisle, assembled overseas from mismatched chicken feathers and too-big plastic feet. Only ten days later, an indigo bunting from the same brood lands on a hummingbird feeder on my porch. It's sleek, fully feathered, and breathtakingly beautiful. Its swollen gape corners have almost disap- peared, and it's flying well (though making a rather bad choice for a perch). It's gone from chipping in the hedge to following its father to the feeders for subsidy. I've read that male indigo buntings can be capricious parents, but this one, identifiable by a small bald spot on his crown, seems to be sticking with his brood.

A walk out to the orchard re- veals a yellow-breasted chat, bill crammed with wobbling caterpillars, on its way to a nest in the hideous tangle of multiflora rose that has grown up under the

Indigo in the rain
5/26/92

Indigo in the rain
5/26/92 Stafford's Fa
MD

dying apples. This pair is one of three that are nesting within earshot of our yard, and yes, we have multiflora rose and even wisteria to thank, in part, for that. A number of lovely native plants have sprung up in the unmown sections of our meadow: spicebush, sumac, sassafras, black raspberry, all thick and unruly, just the way the chats like it. The three males sang throughout late May and June, hooting, cawing, clicking, and sputtering around the clock, but they're quiet now, too busy to sing.

A few hundred feet farther down the orchard path, another pair of indigo buntings is singing the worried song of fledging time. A pair of Kentucky warblers joins them. This is only my second sighting of the warbler this year. I hear them on the tangled slopes below the orchard, but rarely am I so lucky as to see one. Several weeks ago, I found a male, highly agitated, tending a fledgling cowbird. Agitated, I thought with disgust, for all the wrong reasons. He'd been duped into raising another's young. This time, though, I can hear honest-to-goodness baby Kentucky warblers chipping softly in the undergrowth, and my joy at that discovery is underscored by my first sighting of a female Kentucky. She's just like the male, without the black mustache, and she's absolutely beautiful, posing and scolding, all cocked tail and shell pink legs, right next to her resplendent mate.

The babies I'm proudest of, though, besides my own, are the four Carolina wrens that popped out of their nest on the morning of July 4. I'd seen their parents through a cold winter. They slept in an old bluebird box on a shelf in our garage and gladly accepted mealworms on icy days. I expected them to nest somewhere in the garage, but they doubtless judged it too mousy out there for nesting purposes. They raised their first brood in—yep—the multiflora rose tangle in the orchard. As the season wore on and snakes began to rouse themselves, the wrens began to poke about the eaves of our house in search of a safe place for their sec-

Kentucky
warbler nest.

female
Ky. warbler

male- he's got
more black

egg

His song is a loud, rich
Torry-torry-torry- give
from high up, usually
higher than I think to
look!

2nd primary, left
wing

scapular

Screech-
owl feathers
found nearby - yikes!

Ridgepole

ond nest. For two days, the female brought leaves, grass, and rootlets and tried to make the material stay between a crooked downspout and the house siding. It kept sliding off. Under the watchful eye of the wren, I toted a stepladder from the garage and wired a little copper bucket between the downspout and the overhanging eave. It looked like the perfect setup to me—protected from wind, rain, and predators. Obviously, it looked perfect to the wren, too, for she began stuffing it with nesting material even as I was folding the stepladder. Within five hours she had stripped most of the moss from my bonsai tree pots and stuffed it into the copper bucket!

Phoebe and I watched with delight as the wrens fashioned a perfect swirl of moss, flax twigs, animal fur, and my hair—most of the nesting materials I provide on a small table at the edge of the yard. Then they seemed to vanish, but a quick peek revealed that the female was incubating four eggs and all was well. On June 16, the pair began bringing tiny spiders to the hatchlings. Though my references state that most Carolina wrens fledge at around thirteen days, ours lingered in the nest for eighteen and were still tailless when they popped out, little perukes of gray down sticking up above their eyes. They could fly, though, if you can call sputtering ten inches over the ground flying. They're still being fed, twelve days later. I climbed the stepladder again to clean out the nest and found it so perfect, clean, and free of parasites that I couldn't bear to remove it. I'll leave that to the wrens, who may well refurbish it for a third brood or sleep in it this winter.

That copper bucket is a relic of the 1950s. I remember it hanging above our fireplace in Shawnee Mission, Kansas, a potted philodendron, essential houseplant of the era, trailing from it. How it traveled with me through a dozen moves since I left home in 1976 I will never know, but it has surely found its highest use, hole in the bottom, rust and all, in the bend of the downspout, a cradle for Carolina wrens, a repository for blessings.

Going on Vacation

SUMMER IS WANING. Cicadas are playing their lazy saws in the close, humid afternoons. My father always said that meant it was time to go back to school. That phrase still sends a chilly ripple through my psyche, even though I've no school to go back to. I love the cicadas almost as much as I love the rhythmic rasp of katydids. On the night of July 19, it occurred to me that I had not yet heard them, and I drifted off wondering when they would begin. And the night of July 20, they were out in full force, making the dark woods ring with their syncopated beat. My father loved katydid song so much that moving to a part of Iowa that seemed bereft of the insects, he took it upon himself to capture a boxful up north and introduce them. He claimed they were present from that summer on.

Every once in a while, someone in our family will get the bit in her teeth and initiate the rental of a beach house in a concerted effort to get us all together despite the trivialities that keep us apart. The designated date was set, the condos were rented, and nineteen of the Zickefoose clan converged on the Eastern Shore of Delaware to reacquaint ourselves. I approach such summer gatherings with perhaps more trepidation than others, in part because I feed hummingbirds—not just a couple of hummingbirds, but several Tonka truckloads of hummingbirds. And I can't bear the thought that their feeders, so carefully maintained all spring and summer, might go empty.

Here in southern Ohio, we have only ruby-throated hummingbirds, and over the eight years we've lived on Indigo Hill, the population that visits our feeders has built up. And up. Now hummingbirds are darned hard to count at feeders, especially when the rain washes the nectar from flowers and sends them here in droves. They shift and fight and move and switch places so fast that it makes my head spin. A friend from Alabama sent me the Alabama Ornithological Society's newsletter, which contained a piece that interested me greatly. Hummingbird experts Nancy Newfield and Bob and Martha Sargent have joined forces to come up with a formula for counting hummingbirds. Over the years, these dedicated ornithologists have set up nets to band and count the hummingbirds at various feeding stations. They've found that they can band hummingbirds all day and still capture unbanded birds every time they check their nets. They've determined that, if you count all the hummingbirds you can see at one time at your feeder, you can safely

cleaning her foot

Oblong-winged Katydid, ♀
Amblycorypha oblongifolia
October 2, 2005
Call a strident kitzidickkit! like
an elk

multiply that number by *six* to determine how many birds are actually visiting!

I count, with great difficulty, twenty-three ruby-throats at one time at my feeders. You do the math. Suddenly, it became clear to me why I was putting out a half gallon of nectar every morning and usually in the evening, too. After the initial shock wore off, it made perfect sense that perhaps 138 hummingbirds might be using my feeders. Why else would I, who can make a five-pound bag of sugar last three months in wintertime, buy a ten-pounder every time I go to the store? Have a spaghetti pot full of nectar solution on my stove all the time? Why else would I barely have time to let it cool before I have to refill the feeders? Why else would my kitchen counters and floor be distinctly tacky from slopped nectar?

Back to the vacation. A long-suffering friend had offered to care for our birds and fish and bonsais and fancy geraniums, job enough in itself. I don't think she

knew what she was getting into with the hummingbirds, though. The day before we left, in between packing diapers and sun hats and the porta-crib and jars of baby food, I boiled solution. And boiled more solution: eight gallons of nectar, boiled and cooled, and stored in the refrigerator. I bought two more large-capacity hummingbird feeders for a total of five, filled them all, hung them out, and hoped for the best. I'd done all I could, and now it was up to the house sitter. To tell the truth, I was more than ready for a break from cleaning and filling hummingbird feeders. The population had grown so much that it was no longer much fun for me anymore; it was *work*.

Once we finally got out of the house, once the last note was written, the last plant watered, the last burner checked, I breathed a sigh of relief. I loved seeing my family, loved the tribal ritual of passing baby Liam from lap to lap, of watching him and his elder sister, Phoebe, interact with aunts and uncles and cousins. The beach community we went to, though, had been so thoroughly inundated with humans for so long that not much remained but sand and water.

Everything that could possibly interest me as a naturalist had been removed from this stretch of shoreline. All the flotsam and jetsam, the countless little miracles and mysteries of the tide wrack, were raked away like so much trash, and with them the food base for any shorebirds. One morning, with Phoebe dabbling in the surf with cousins and Liam safely in my sister's arms, I decided to walk until I saw a shorebird. One, two miles went by under my feet, and I saw a break in the endless beach umbrellas and a little strip of dune vegetation that was a nature reserve. It was so small I could see where the umbrellas started on its other side, but I decided to investigate. Standing between the sparse beach grass and the waterline were a confused-looking willet and a just-fledged Forster's tern. Both dodged the stream of walkers as best they could, and both soon flew off without finding anything to eat.

Zinnias
in the sun

I lay down on the comparatively empty beach of the reserve and contemplated what we've made of our shoreline. We've sanitized it, smoothed it out, paved it over, taken even the plant life away. It might as well be a big public pool. I marveled that the waves still broke on this unnatural shore. Their rhythm soothed my roiling mind, and I watched brown pelicans coast by, then closed my eyes. From far away, the drone of a biplane broke the silence, growing louder and louder as it bore down on this strip of sand so thick with humanity. I cracked an eye toward the blinding light and saw that it bore an advertising banner for a bar. It was closely followed by a second, then a third, then a fourth biplane, each trailing a banner. Now even the sound of nature had been drowned out. It was a clean sweep. I longed for our backwoods home, where nature dominates, rules, runs my day. I'd be thrilled to hear the drone of hummingbird wings. That evening, my mother sensed my misery. "A vacation is to make you appreciate home," she said. How true.

Home again. The house sitter sounded frazzled on the phone and I knew why. The hummingbird numbers had fallen off a bit, but there were still at least a dozen around. I dove into the feeder maintenance with renewed energy. I hopped on my little green tractor and mowed the lawn, then weeded the gardens and pulled up the green beans. There'd been plenty of rain while we were gone, so I replanted. I picked a bouquet of zinnias and put them on the kitchen table in a cobalt vase. Home. It was so good to be home. I heard a tap on the kitchen window and glanced up. The male sharp-shinned hawk who keeps me a little bit on edge all the time had developed a new trick in our absence. Turning on a dime, with five cents change, he whipped up to a hummingbird feeder, plucked a bird off a perch, and exited. That was a first. I wondered what else had happened out my kitchen window while we were gone. I'd just have to stay put and keep watching.

Wren Wranch

"YOU...DON'T...ALWAYS...*HAVE*...TO...KNOW!" Bill hollered each word, punctuating his shouts with the sliding clanks of our twelve-foot extension ladder as he folded it back up. *You're right*, I thought as I dusted bits of Spanish moss off my shirt. *But just in case, keep that ladder handy.*

As I think back on this summer, I will remember it as the one when the Carolina wrens worked their way deep into my heart (as well as into every nook and cranny around the house). I think there were three and a half pairs living within a stone's throw of our front door; two honest pairs and one male, who I'm pretty sure was squiring two mates. Keeping track of even seven Carolina wrens necessitates a lot of note taking and cross checking of those notes. I'll never know for sure how many adults nested here, but by summer's end, I was determined to get an accurate count of all the young they produced. Hence the ladder.

I found my first clutch on April 11, incubation well under way in a tidy nest tucked into a stash of plastic grocery bags in the recycling depository in our garage. I was gathering the bags up to recycle them in town when a little brown bullet spurted out, diving under my elbow. I abandoned the effort, leaving the nest undisturbed. The female sat on her eggs stoically, hatching four young. When they were twelve days old, I noticed the male wren visiting a little copper bucket I'd

Two (presumably ♀)
Carolina wrens fight,
pecking each others' vents, while
the male sings vigorously. They
eventually nested 50' apart, one
under the bark, one in the garage.
The male fed both broods. Polygamy in
a genetically monogamous species!

wired up under the eaves by our front door. Ladder time. Another nest, with five three-day-old babies!

Lulled by the presence of the pair in the garage only fifty feet away, I hadn't even known there was another active nest! There had to be two females. I'd seen the same male feed the babies in the garage, then fly up to the copper bucket nest. My mind flew back to March 29, when a third wren had appeared in the yard and been involved in a vicious fight with one member of the resident pair. They rolled over and over, pecking each other's vents. It was the avian equivalent of a catfight. Now, I guessed, the newcomer was the second female, the one who had laid her eggs, unnoticed, in an old nest in the copper bucket.

Both nests fledged uneventfully, bringing the total to nine fledglings. The garage female started a new nest in a joint compound bucket hanging from a nail ten days after the first brood fledged. Five fledged from her second joint compound bucket nest. There were fourteen young from these three adults so far and it was only June 20. I couldn't wait to see what our season total would be. But it was getting confusing. A nest appeared in a hanging basket right by the front door on July 2. The garage was deserted. I couldn't be sure which female was responsible. Three more young fledged from the hanging basket. By July 20, the count was seventeen, not bad for three adults.

Just down the hill in our backyard, I find a Carolina wren nest with five eggs in a nest box meant for titmice and chickadees. Five fledge on the eighth of July. Twenty-two baby wrens. I'm glad I've been keeping notes, though I have to admit I have no idea whether this box-nesting pair has anything to do with the three adults nesting around the house. I think we have to be done. And then, on the fifth of August, Bill spots a Carolina wren, identity and partner unknown, stuffing moss into a three-sided phoebe nesting shelter twenty feet up under an eave on the back side of the house. I lug the extension ladder out and find four more eggs. Holy smokes! By the twentieth of August, I just HAVE TO KNOW how many young are in that nest. Ladder time again. I wobble to the very top while Bill holds the ladder beneath me. I peer into the nest and I can't see anything. If I were smart, I'd realize that's because all four baby wrens have their eyes screwed shut and are flattened into the nest lining. But I have to poke a tentative finger in to lower the nest rim and see what's inside. That's when the nest explodes in my face. Baby wrens flutter to the ground and hop off in four directions. Bill and Phoebe scurry frantically to catch them. They hand them back up to me. I stuff them back in the nest four times. A couple are still in pinfeathers. This is not good. Let's see. I can stand up here holding the babies down until nightfall, or I can come up with something better right now.

I yell down to Bill as I'm holding all four down in the nest for the fourth time to go get me a big wad of dry Spanish moss from my potting supplies. With one hand I slip it over the frightened babies, slide my other hand out, then cautiously fashion an entrance to the newly domed nest so the parents can slip in and feed the babies. A baby wren immediately shoots out of the hole and hits me in the nose. *Good thing my mouth was closed.* By now I am laughing helplessly and in real danger of falling off the ladder. Bill catches the bird and hands it back up to me. I poke it back into the nest, hold my hand over the entry tunnel for a minute or two until the babies stop cheeping and popping around, then carefully climb back down the ladder. Bill silently lifts the ladder away from the house, carrying it back to the garage before he folds it and hollers his frustration at my inquisitiveness.

"YOU . . . DON'T . . . ALWAYS . . . *HAVE* . . . TO . . . KNOW!" (*Oh, but I do. I'm*

Adapt of the
Wren Wranch,
2002

sorry, honey, but you knew I was a science monkey when you married me.) Against all odds and expectations, my baby wren containment system works. The parents, whoever they are, are still feeding the young in the nest when they fledge on time, two days later: numbers 23, 24, 25, and 26. Never were numbers written in a spiral notebook with more satisfaction and relief. Whewww. I can't wait to see what next season holds for the Wren Wranch.

FALL

Grey fox, ♂ Gallagher's Fork
November 17, 2003 *signature*
catching grasshoppers in
the main path

Chicken Fever

The Harvard rooster Day 2

When I saw the tiny pink comb on his crown, I couldn't leave him at the Biolabs.

HERE'S WHAT I WANT: chickens. I've *always* wanted chickens. But chickens, like horses, need special housing, more specifically a coop and a pen, and that's why, in part, I've never had them. Well, when I was a freshman in college, I did raise a lovely leghorn chick, one I'd kidnapped from a lab, where it was about to undergo experiments on its eyes. I saw the tiny pink comb emerging from the cocoa brown stripes on its little head and I couldn't bear to think of its going under the knife. I asked the professor if I might have it, and he assented. Being newly hatched, it imprinted on me as its mother and followed me wherever I went, a chicken in Harvard Yard. Thinking back on it, I believe that I, with my overalls, tailbone-length hair, and imprinted chicken, was admitted to that institution for comic relief. Later I would add roller skates to the mix, but by then the chicken was long gone.

I raised it until it was a lanky, freely pooping adolescent rooster. My suite mates were nonplussed; he lived in our common room and was pleasant enough as long as I kept his papers fresh. Then he began to croon and moan, and I knew midnight crowing could not be far behind. Before he found his voice, I would have to find him a real home, and I was determined that it not be a laboratory. I asked around the administrative offices until I found a woman with a weekend farm in New Hampshire. She told me that her flock rooster was getting old and that this one would do nicely. What a relief. I packed him into a cardboard box and left him with her on a Friday afternoon. Having a harem sure beats donating your lenses to science.

Chicken fever reached a pitch by the time the county fair rolled around in September. I couldn't bear to look at the white meat chickens, with their huge breast muscles and stocky legs. Like the turkeys, they looked maladapted, over-weight, and miserable. No, I stared at the show bantams in their tiny cages like a car fanatic at an auto show, taking in every detail, every finely penciled feather and glossy hackle. The silver Sebright laid me low. M. C. Escher couldn't have in-vented a more beautiful chicken. Every silvery white feather was rimmed in glossy black, creating a lacy pattern over its body, flowing over and defining its compact curves . . . rhapsody.

Most people, I suspect, want chickens for one of two things: meat or eggs. The question of offing my chickens for meat would, for me, be akin to murder. Once you've named something, raised it from a chick, how do you . . .? I know that sounds silly to anyone who's been raised on a farm, but I'm after their souls, their aesthetics, not their drumsticks. I could eat their eggs, I know, and since we run through almost two dozen a week (thank you, Dr. Atkins!), I could probably ra-tionalize investing in a flock by saying we need the eggs. Eggs. South American Araucanas lay glossy eggs in shivery shades of jade and sea foam. Martha Stewart

Silver Sebrights
at the fair
September 3 '05

claims that her interior decorating colors were inspired by the eggs her flock lays. I believe it.

Signs began to appear to me, signs that told me it was time to build a coop. I opened my *USA Today*, only to find an article crowing, "City Slickers Click with

Backyard Cluckers." Ah. Definitely a sign. Bill brought a book home from work titled *Extraordinary Chickens*. It's at my bedside. Porno for chicken fanatics. Even my dear high school English teacher, who made me into a writer, egged me on. "There is something comforting," she wrote, about chickens "roaming about, making soothing noises as if they just discovered some wonderful thing right there in the dirt they scratched up—quite oblivious to the horrors outside of their realm. I think they'll fit right in."

a pullet. There are already echoes of the hen in her face.
Tractor Supply 3/05

I solicited advice from an old friend from high school, who knows my tendency toward tenderness. "When I had chickens, one of them outsmarted me. He used reverse psychology on me. Whenever I went out to catch one to whack for dinner, instead of running away he would come right up to me. I would always pass him over and go chop another one. It finally came down to him and two females. I figured I'd keep the male, since he was so nice, and pick one of the females for his bride. I carefully scrutinized the females. One of them had a crooked foot. *Whap!* That was all for her. So the male and his lucky girlfriend hung around the barn and got bigger and bigger and bigger."

Bigger and bigger, and older and older, I thought. The other obstacle, besides the coop and pen hurdles, that I haven't figured out how to cross is the aging hen factor. I know that I'll get attached to these birds, as my friend Nell in Connecticut did to hers. When I lived in Connecticut, I did a lot of songbird rehabilitation, and Nell used to bring me wild birds that her barn cats had roughed up. Sometimes I'd have to put a bird down if it was too badly injured to rehabilitate. Nell took note of that. One day, she showed up in my driveway with a trunk full of old laying hens.

"I wondered if you'd put my old hens down for me. I'm attached to them, and they aren't laying anymore, but I can't bear to kill them."

I stared at her in silence, thinking about what to say. "That," I said, "is why I don't have chickens." I sent her off to the pharmacy for ether and advised her to kill her own darn old chickens.

I know why I want chickens. I figured it out on my son Liam's second day of preschool. Bill drove away with both kids, for once, in the car and school bound, and I was alone with the silence of a house, all to myself. It was heaven, but it was too quiet. This revelation took me completely by surprise, but I knew it was real. I need something else to care for. The orchids and greenhouse and bonsais and gardens and aquarium and fishpond and macaw and bird feeders and hummingbirds and house and husband and (momentarily absent) kids just aren't enough.

I'm waiting for the fever to pass. When my daughter, Phoebe, started first grade, I suddenly wanted a retired racing greyhound. Now a racing greyhound on our place makes about as much sense as a pet giraffe. Deer, rabbits, woodchucks, chipmunks, raccoons, opossums, skunks—they all waltz through our front yard like they own the place, and a sight-hunting hound like that would leave a dog-shaped hole in the front screen door lighting out after them and never be seen again. If I could ever catch it, I'd be left with walking the fool thing on a lead when we've got eighty acres for any dog with a crumb of sense to wander at will. But it had to be a racing greyhound or nothing. Suffice it to say I got over it, mostly. I stay away from the greyhound Web sites, especially the one that plays "Someone to Watch Over Me" as you scroll tearfully down the photo gallery of otherwise doomed hounds up for adoption.

Now it's chickens. I've *always* wanted chickens.

Chicks underway

The Turning of the Year

PERHAPS IT IS FITTING, on the night of the first hard frost, when everything outside is dying, to be thinking about death. Not in a morbid way, but in a philosophical way, as a sad but necessary thing. The cold ushers in death to so many things I love, things I've grown all summer. Lately I feel so acutely attuned to the rhythms of the season that I feel the chlorophyll pulling out of the leaves. Today, knowing that frost was coming, I saved everything I could. (I do fight death, when I can, to cheat Winter of her dreary little victories.) Phoebe and I gathered nine fat monarch caterpillars from our little milkweed ranch and brought them inside for the night, unwilling to chance losing them to this unseasonable frost. I lifted huge pots of upright fuchsia, little pots of impatiens and fancy dwarf geraniums, my rosemary tree that's as old as Phoebe and brushing my chin now, a perfect Christmas tree, twice as aromatic as a fir. I loaded them all in the garden cart, shoved them into my little greenhouse, and cranked the gas heat up. Already reigning supreme inside is my gardenia, a sprawling shrub that can't be cut back, for it's got a bud or a flower on every tip. That scent alone will get me through the winter. Oh, darn. Forgot to get the heliotrope in. Ah, well, I'm out of room, anyway. But I'll be kicking myself in January, when its vanilla scent would be filling the greenhouse. Maybe I'll dig it up before I go to bed. I must have heliotrope in midwinter. *Remember to dig that heliotrope, Zick.*

I like to feed birds year-round. I especially love it in summer, when the indigo bunting daubs its blue among a dozen yellow goldfinches and the scarlet swatches of cardinals right on the deck outside the living room. The kids watch them all day long, and Liam waits for the chipmunk (he calls it a "squirelt") so he can call me to come shoo it away before it vacuums up the last of the sunflower hearts. "Mommy! That bad lil' squirelt is back!" He knows he'll get a kiss out of it, not to mention the spectacle of his mother chasing a chipmunk down two flights of stairs while roaring like a lion. Dumb, but effective.

Along about the first of August, I noticed a swelling on the eye of our female chipping sparrow. Soon her eye was so swollen as to be useless, and she swiveled her head around to peek at us with her good eye. That eye was soon afflicted, too, and an exam through binoculars suggested that she had a bad case of avian pox. This herpes-like virus is highly contagious—not something you want at your bird feeder, especially in summer, when things are warm and moist and fecund. What to do? She was feeding a fledged youngster that was too young to find food on its own. I cut down the amount of food I put out every day, so it would be sure to disappear before night, and watched. Within a week, the fledgling was eating on its own and its mother was so weak she could barely feed herself. I knew the time would come when she would be unable to fly, and then it would be up to me to ease her passage.

I've never been able to turn away from creatures that are dying badly. I guess it's all the songbird rehabilitation I've done over the years. I know too well what awaits the sick ones when night falls.

I found the female chippy at sunrise, huddled on the patio, where she had probably spent the night. Gently, I wrapped her in a paper towel, made her comfortable in a small plastic container, and gave her a quick puff of car exhaust. It was over in seconds. This wretched disease would only spread if the carcass stayed outdoors. Avian pox virus stays alive six months or more in a carcass.

I wondered about her apparently healthy fledgling, but a week hadn't passed before I found it, nearly blinded by pox, making its feeble way toward the birdbath. Sadly, I gave it the same quiet end as its mother. I started a fire with a pile of newspapers and burned the fledgling's carcass, as I had its mother's, then went inside, feeling low, to look at the deck feeder. It was time to stop feeding the birds.

How I would miss my bunting, my goldfinches, the tame cardinals that brightened each dawn and dusk. But I knew that the wooden feeder had to be taken out of service.

Heliotrope in the greenhouse February 8 2005

Heliotrope likes cool roots. Within days of being repotted, it flourished and burst into bloom. It has a spicy cherry-vanilla scent that's essential to my winter. What a wonderful plant. Even the flowers are quilted. Whitefly and aphids love it as much as I do.

Bill and I scrubbed everything—feeders, stands, deck, and railing—with bleach solution, rinsed it all, and left it to dry in the sun. We stored the feeders and stands in the garage for a month and a half, and I tried to ignore the goldfinches and mourning doves that peered in the windows at me, wondering why I no longer popped out at first light to spread their feast.

The birds that had once crowded my feeders dispersed, as they should, and the yard was eerily quiet. Driving up the driveway, walking up the sidewalk, it occurred to me that now it was like anyone else's yard. No rush of wings greeted me when I came home, no twitters, no song, other than the odd call from the woods or shrubby borders. It hit me how profoundly my feeding program had changed things. I missed my friends mightily, but I knew I owed them a chance to escape this dreadful disease.

Cold brings death to my gardens, but it also kills or renders dormant many of the viruses and bacteria that thrive in summer. When the air finally took a snap and October approached, I couldn't stand the silence any longer. I took the scrubbed feeders and stands out and put a few handfuls of seed in them. It took a couple of weeks to regain a regular clientele, and I searched their faces for any sign of pox. They all looked beautiful, bright-eyed, and healthy. My friends were back and the world was right again. Even the "bad lil' squirelt" was back, filling its oral carpetbags with expensive sunflower hearts. Liam hollered for me, then looked at me with twinkling eyes, waiting for the show. We were having fun again.

Oh, yeah—the heliotrope. Need my trowel and a pot. Pajamas, clogs, trowel, pot—dug, done. All right, Winter. Bring it on.

The Vultures Knew

Anderson Specials, Sungolds, Tendergreen and Brittle Wax beans Sept 14 2005

HERE'S THE TYPICAL Ohio Valley summer.
The sun shines, and it rains a little in the spring, just
enough to make you think you'll be able to grow a good garden. Fooled, you
throw yourself into your vegetables. They grow wonderfully. You get some lettuce,
some beans. The sun keeps shining. You get a tomato or two. It shines until everything dries up and gets crispy. It keeps shining. A cloud doesn't pass over its face
again until after the first frost. Then it rains and rains and rains, like a waiter who
says as you're paying the check, parched and furious, "I'm sorry, you asked for
more water? I was busy at another table. Here's your water."

In the fall and winter, it's gray all the time. Tough weather for turkey vultures,
who like a good sunny day and some thermals to lift them high above the hills. So
it was with interest that I watched them circling, swooping, beating their great
sable wings low over my yard for three days running, defying the low ceiling and
soggy skies. Eight in all. *There must be something good down in the woods,* I thought, *or
they wouldn't bother getting off their roost in this weather . . .*

Even though the weather is usually iffy in mid-October, the Big Sit is probably our favorite organized bird watching event. It falls just at the time of year when we start to cocoon, with sweaters and soups and oatmeal cookies. We invite friends and acquaintances to our bird watching tower—which tops our house like the stack of an ocean liner—to sit for all or part of a twelve-hour shift, simply identifying every bird that flies by, trying to get a bigger list of species than last year. We talk and laugh and act silly and eat, and we try to outdo each other with outlandish sightings. It's perfectly tailored to our relaxed (slothful) approach to birding.

The neat thing about the Big Sit is that when you sit looking over the landscape for twelve hours on an October day, you can see almost anything. This year (2002) was the best we'd ever had—the biggest list, the best friends joining us from afar, and the most amazing sightings. Fifty red-tailed hawks, maybe two hundred turkey vultures, a harrier. Red-headed woodpeckers. A small, distant flock of what could only be snow geese appeared, then disappeared, chimerae on the horizon. At dusk, six black-crowned night herons, species number 178 for our property, rowed by against a burnished orange backdrop. We whooped, we crowed, we slapped high fives all around. But we weren't done. It was almost completely dark when a great blue heron flapped over, barely visible but voicing its distinguishing croak. Number 61 for the day.

"Hoot, Zick, hoot!" Bill urged, and I wound up my barred owl imitation. Before I'd made all eight hoots, one, two, then a third barred owl answered from the valleys to the north and south. Sixty-two species, a new Big Sit record for our sanctuary and home. We had great birds, great company, and great food. The perfect bird watching event.

Bill takes the Sit seriously, enough so that he drove straight from New York City the night of October 12 in order to be in the tower at dawn on the thirteenth.

I put out the road-killed
coon I'd used for a painting
10/29 and by that afternoon
these splendid creatures showed
up to take advantage
plus Jane 10/30/92 White Hall

Since he was traveling this year, it was up to me to assemble the snacks. I will confess I neglected to buy the caffeinated cola, nacho cheese–flavored tortilla chips, French onion potato chips, and flame orange cheese puffs that he'd scribbled on the shopping list and which he considers part of the essential Big Sit diet. It's not that I'm a food snob, but I make a point of whizzing by the snack and soda aisles and I couldn't bring myself to buy those things. All right, I'm an unrepentant food snob. I would make healthy food for our guests, and Bill wasn't here to argue. I'd cook all day Saturday and be ready to bird all day Sunday. Hang the cheese puffs.

I ran down a mental list. A chicken stew with carrots, white kidney beans, and kale from the garden, topped with fresh Parmesan. Fresh-baked baguettes. Oatmeal raisin cookies (an essential). Who could pine for cheese puffs? I went down to the basement refrigerator to collect my stewing chicken, bought and stored four days earlier. And it was not there. *Hmm. I know I bought a chicken. I'll check upstairs again.* And I went off to other tasks, meaning to check later.

A pile of mail by the door beckoned. I'd drive it out to the box quickly before the mailman came. I opened the garage door and noticed a foul odor. *Phew, I've got to take that garbage to town.* I opened the door of my Explorer and reeled backward. *Something died in here!*

Gingerly, I lifted the back hatch and saw the small white grocery bag, forgotten, in the near corner. My chicken, its thick plastic wrapping swollen to near bursting, had been

10/30/92
Waiting for the raccoon to settle

Silver underwings
reflect the snow
beautifully

1/11/88 Dolbia

a 25° fresh snowy day
bright and shining

like Ciconiiformes, a see-thru
nostril

Tired but couldn't swallow
the grass's head

bill bone white
head livid red w/
white carunctes and
black fuzz on nape
a s has hallux in wrinkled folds

4/11/88 Dolbia

2 brought in by an
old filet of blue, a roadkilled
ruffed grouse, chicken guts
and a windowkilled mourning
dove. The 1st flew off with the
board-frozen fish in its bill and
ate in the woods, the second suffered crows pulling its
frayed wingtips' to eat grouse and dove

stewing in the warm garage for the past week. Chickens almost always leak. I owe a thank-you letter to the packager, because this one hadn't, not a drop. The damage was purely olfactory.

I eased the bag out by its handles as one might lift a live grenade or a box trap with a very angry skunk inside. I backed out of the garage, holding the noisome bolus at arm's length. Four vultures trained knowing eyes on me as I carried it ceremoniously out to the wooden post in the middle of our meadow, where I leave freezer-burned treasures and the occasional roadkill for their enjoyment.

I retreated to the house to wash up and laugh. I dug some chicken legs out of the freezer and started them stewing for the soup. The vultures circled and tilted low over the Explorer, which was airing out, its doors and windows ajar, in the driveway. All eight of them, the same pack that had been trying all week to tell me where that chicken was.

Letting It Go

Basil *Ocimum basilicum*

THE AIR IS COOLING. On the Weather Channel, perky Muzak accompanies the red and blue fronts that sweep in from Canada and the Rockies, bringing wave after wave of blustery cold and little flocks of the birds of wintertime. Yesterday, juncos visited the feeding station for the first time, looking a little out of place on the still-verdant lawn. The dozen house sparrows that don't seem to grasp how much I dislike them were joined by an impossibly elegant adult white-crowned sparrow. It looked like an art student in the dusky rabble of pecking house sparrows, wearing a jaunty

black-and-white beret tipped over its eyes, as it stripped the crabgrass seeds in my overgrown lawn.

I wind down my gardening efforts, letting tomatoes ripen and drop from the tired vines, letting the basil go to seed as it has striven to do all summer. I canned tomatoes this summer, shocked to find that the price of twelve jars of herbed tomato sauce is an entire day of standing by the stove: seven hours of chopping and skinning and stirring, dunking, sterilizing, and washing. Salsa is even more work, but I know that come January, the fragrant hiss of a just-opened jarful of summer will be worth every minute of it. The garden, right in front of my kitchen window, stands in glorious disorder, awash in sprawling tomatoes, springing with crabgrass and overflowing nasturtiums and marigolds, proud zinnias still barely holding their heads above it all. Rustling and peeping and sorting through the tangle are the birds of summer, the birds of autumn, the birds of winter.

All summer long, the common yellowthroats and blue-gray gnatcatchers, and even a family of yellow-breasted chats, used the garden as their insect larder, gleaning the bean leaves and spooking through the tomatoes, sallying out after flying prey from the tall pea fence that lines the back of the raised beds. Bluebirds were a constant presence on the fence and on the special sticks and snags we erected as perches for them all around the lawn. And now that fall is here, the shifts are changing. Chipping sparrows and yellow-rumped, palm, and Cape May warblers—the birds of autumn—flit and pinwheel through the vines. They will not stay the winter with us, but while they're here, they find the wreck of our garden irresistible. It bears fruit beyond edibles; it's alive with birds every morning. Winter residents—eastern towhees and field, white-throated, and song sparrows; cardinals, juncos, goldfinches—have been stripping the flower heads since the first seed

Cottontail, hiding
in the meadow's edge

formed, and they'll continue to find food here until early April, when I clear the beds and dig a furrow for planting peas.

My gardening style isn't for everyone, and there are some cases where cleanliness is the better route. If you've had trouble with rust, wilt, black spot, and other fungal diseases, especially in beans, tomatoes, and roses, it's best to remove and burn the plants at season's end. Whatever you do, don't just toss them on the compost heap—the spores will survive the winter to infest next year's plants. Just before frost, my tea roses, the "greeters" by the front stoop, put on a last spectacular show of big fragrant blooms, having fought black spot all summer long. Ironically, city roses seem not to suffer as much black spot, for the polluted air kills off the fungus! But out here in the country, where the living ought to be easier, the roses make set after set of leaves as black spot causes them to fall. Fungicides and pesticides aren't in my gardening repertoire. I said my gardening style isn't for everyone—it's for the birds.

As I watch my gardens flourish, I take note of which plants seem particularly useful to birds and butterflies. A mild winter in 1997–98 let the buddleia bushes keep their leaves until March, when a hard freeze finally wilted them. Then I cut the shrubs back to about knee-high, which, done in springtime, will stimulate new growth. As I write, seven months later, they're twelve feet high and covered in the last flush of lavender bloom before frost. All summer, the fritillaries and swallowtails, red admirals and painted ladies jostled for space with ruby-throated hummingbirds on those drooping clusters of fragrant blossoms. I had never seen hummingbirds give buddleia more than a cursory poke before this summer, when the feeding fad caught on. Now the huge bushes will give good cover to winter birds before it's time to cut them back again in the spring.

I let it all stand and slowly collapse in on itself, this wreck of a vegetable gar-

190 *Letters from Eden*

den. I know to some it looks trashy, but put a white-crowned sparrow against the weedy backdrop and you have something that but for the trash, you'd never see. Zinnias and coneflowers, blasted by frost, are sad and black, like burned skeletons, but top one with a goldfinch and they're not so sad anymore. I don't deny that my flower beds look awful all winter and well into the spring, but I find beauty hiding there just beneath the surface, scratching on the ground, rattling the spent stem.

Avian Intelligence

IT IS A WINTER DAY, and I am standing in the weak lemon sun in Harvard Square, in Cambridge, Massachusetts, waiting to cross a busy street. I look south, down Massachusetts Avenue, and see a city bus approaching. There is a squadron of pigeons accompanying it, flying at the level of the windows. My curiosity is piqued, and I wait out the light to see what happens. An elderly woman slowly climbs down the bus steps. She carries a cane and a shopping bag. The pigeons descend on her, fluttering noisily as she makes her way to a bench outside my freshman dorm. I'm not surprised to see her pull bread and peanuts from the shopping bag and begin scattering them to her clattery brood. I turn to a passerby who has watched the whole scene with me. "She's here every day at the same time. The birds follow her bus from Boston." I wonder how it all evolved, how the pigeons learned her schedule, her route from her home to the square. And then I realize that for a species renowned for its precise homing powers, this is a small feat. Peanuts, in fact.

Years later, I am renting a small beach cottage in Old Lyme, Connecticut, for the fall. I love fall at the shore, with its biting winds and pounding surf, its leaden skies and keening gulls. I seem to be in the minority. The neighborhood is deserted, its uninsulated cottages empty. Crows patrol the lonely beach. Tame crows. I seize the opportunity to befriend them and start laying leftovers out on the lawn. I delight in watching the big sable birds caching their treasures in the grass, covering them carefully with wads of sod. My beef stew is a huge hit. Chunks are buried everywhere.

The crows quickly learn who the Food Lady is. One afternoon, I'm returning from town in my little silver car when I see a crow suddenly reverse its northerly flight to follow me south. Then another follows, and another. I'm still a mile or more from the cottage. The crows make the right turn into my development and begin to caw lustily as I turn in to the driveway. Not only do they recognize me, but they know my little Colt, and they know when I'm home and when I'm not, and they watch for my return. They've made their point. I head straight for the refrigerator to reinforce their behavior.

The beach crows return the favor every day, gracing me with their presence. I even got a nice pair of sunglasses from them. Two individuals were tussling on the sand, obviously in play, passing a piece of driftwood back and forth. One gripped the wood in its foot, an unusual feat for corvids, which, as a family, generally carry objects only in their bills. It tried to walk while carrying the stick, then flopped over onto its side and rolled onto its back, passing the wood from one foot to the other. The second crow stole it and they wrestled like two pups for a

while. A third crow flew in, carrying a pair of sunglasses in its bill, and the game of keep-away continued, with the glasses as the prize. When they were through playing, I picked up the sunglasses. I've long since lost the glasses, but I remember my crow friends and wonder if they remember me. Chances are . . .

Birds remember. They notice. They observe carefully. It's in their job description to do it. We don't take much notice of their everyday behavior as a rule; we don't give much thought to whether intelligence is involved in it. When those natural avian aptitudes intersect with our lives, though, we deem them intelligent. In short, the more birds behave like us, the smarter we think they must be.

The ornithological literature is rich with examples of "presumed intelligent" behavior in birds. The American (and Japanese) barn swallows who learned to hover before an electric eye and open the warehouse door that would gain them access to their nesting place. The crows who dropped walnuts into a busy intersection, watched the car tires crush them, then waited for a red light to go collect the meats. The green herons who use twigs, feathers, and even fish food to bait their prey. I love reading these accounts, and I revel in the oh-so-careful objective descriptions of the observers as they step around the question of whether a bird could truly demonstrate intelligent behavior. And I take great pleasure in collecting some examples of my own. Some have even been deemed of scientific merit.

My then-two-year-old nephew Evan and I were happily flaunting the rules one autumn day, feeding ducks and geese at a lake in my mother's retirement community in Richmond, Virginia. We'd no sooner pulled out the plastic bread bags than a great blue heron spread its slaty wings and made a beeline across the lake to our side. Barely ten feet away, it stood on the shore, looking out of hard yellow eyes at us. It clearly wanted something. Never having been approached by a great blue heron before, I thought fast and tossed it a piece of bread. It grabbed the bread and ate it. How strange. I hadn't thought herons liked bread. I tossed a second piece. It picked it up, then dropped it, and kept looking at us. I tossed the next piece into the water, and the heron stepped quickly toward it as the geese hurried to get out of its way. Now we were getting somewhere. The heron stood staring into the water beneath the floating bread, then stabbed, bringing up a fat, flipping bluegill. It moved back to the shore to process and swallow its catch headfirst, then waded back into the water. While it was away, the geese had stolen its bread. The heron turned its head and looked at me again. I tossed more bread to it until four pieces floated around beneath it.

The geese, emboldened by hunger, drew closer to the heron. It struck at them when they tried to snatch the floating bread. In the course of only twenty minutes, the heron caught three bluegills that were attracted to its bait. When the bread was gone, the heron packed it in and flew off, leaving me to search the literature for any other examples of bait fishing in great blue herons. It's a behavior that's well known in green herons and only recently described in tricolored herons and

The Summerhill heron, fishing with bait

black-crowned night herons. There were no accounts in the literature, and my friend Ted Davis, a professor at Boston University, helped me write up the incident for *Colonial Waterbirds* [J. Zickefoose and W. E. Davis, Jr., "Great Blue Heron (*Ardea herodias*) Uses Bread as Bait for Fish," 21:87–88]. From the speed with which the heron approached us and then left us when the bread ran out, I doubt it was the first time it had fished with bread for bait. Happily for the science of ornithology, it chose a bread supplier with a special interest in bait-fishing herons!

It's unlikely that the great blue heron learned this behavior by watching other herons. Green herons, a favorite bird of my childhood in Richmond, are vanishingly hard to come by now, and they don't inhabit the lake this bird frequented. What is more likely is that the heron noticed that fish are attracted to the feeding frenzy when geese are given bread, and then made the mental leap to station itself near bread, protect the bread, and reap the benefits. Not bad for a bird whose brain is probably half the size of a kiwi fruit.

Putting two and two together—the basic hallmark of intelligence. One of my favorite stories concerns ospreys. I was sketching them one summer, stationed at a nest platform just off a dock near Old Black Point, Connecticut. A neighbor noticed me there day after day and came down to talk. We commented on how quickly the birds had acclimated to my presence; after perhaps twenty minutes of cheeping and circling on my initial visit, they accepted me as harmless and went about their business for that and subsequent sessions. Since his house overlooked the nest, the ospreys had acclimated to his presence—unless . . . "If I come out the front door and walk down to my mailbox, they don't say a thing. But as soon as they see me put my boots on, they start yelling. I put my boots on way up by the front door, but they know that means I'm going to take the boat out. My boat is moored right next to their nest and they don't like my messing around there. And they yell at me from the minute I put my boots on until I'm out in the channel." Told this story, osprey researcher and aficionado Paul Spitzer chortled, "Those birdies, they're not as dumb as they look!"

These are only a few of my favorite anecdotes of bird intelligence. They're not particularly unusual or amazing, but they're mine. And then there is the story of Lewis, a yellow-naped Amazon parrot belonging to my friends writers Jane and Michael Stern. They entrusted me with her care once while they were away on an

extended research trip. Now, Lewis talks, but she's not what you might call gifted. She shouts and sings and whistles, but she's usually far from putting together a cogent phrase. This particular morning, I left her alone while I was preparing her breakfast. When I entered the room, she was pirouetting around on a table with a razor-blade paint scraper in her beak. Her crown and nape feathers were raised to the fullest, her chartreuse tail flared. "Oh-oh!" she crowed. "Don't play with that!" I nearly dropped my tray. When Jane and Michael returned, they told me that upon being taken from her carrier on her first day in their home, she looked around the room and asked in a soft voice, "Where am I?" She'd never said either phrase before and never said either one again.

There is probably an explanation somewhere for Lewis's appropriate use of English phrasing in these situations. Perhaps on some other similar occasion she heard someone say the phrases with enough emphasis that they "stuck" in her brain, and she recalled them in the excitement of the moment. I'd like to leave open the possibility that something wonderful happened inside that little parrot's head, for something wonderful surely happened in mine.

Birding with Bambinos

OH, LORD, I had better pour another glass of Escudo Rojo. I took my two-year-old, Liam, birding with me this afternoon. I need hardly mention that Phoebe, five, was along; she's only additive in such a situation.

It started innocently enough. Fresh off a trip to south Texas, where Bill and I birded and partied and hawked our respective wares at the Rio Grande Valley Birding Festival in Harlingen, Phoebe always by our side, I guess I was under the delusion that one could and should take the bambinos along. Phoebe's no problem, cheerily allowing herself to be hoisted to scope level to peer at the bird of the moment and always able to amuse herself with markers and paper. She'd stalk butterflies and repeat their names as we identified them for her, collect shells and pretty rocks, try strange foods in restaurants. We'd take her to the end of the earth. Liam, on the other hand, stayed home with a trusted sitter.

Liam is Phoebe's evil twin. To be fair to him, he's just turned two, but he's truly a different ball of wax, the anti-Phoebe. People witness his tirades and say, "The terrible twos, huh?" and I wearily reply, "The terrible ones, twos . . ." I'm the same mom who raised Phoebe; if anything, more experienced and relaxed and sane than I was the first time around. I'm home with him virtually all the time, leaping to satisfy his every need before his ranting rises to fever pitch. According to my mother, I was just such a baby. Implicit in that comment is the hint that I somehow *deserve* this fussy bundle.

And yet . . . I wouldn't trade him for the best-behaved baby in the land. I am completely in love with him, his bowl of white hair, his ice blue eyes, his nimble little hands. He's preverbal, prone to frustration at my dimwittedness when I can't figure out what he wants. Most of the time, I can redirect his attention to his farm set, his trains, his beloved macaw, his favorite videos, and peace reigns. All bets are off, though, when we leave the comforting environs of home.

Right after lunch, I strapped the kids into the Explorer and set off, scope and sketch pad on the seat beside me. An immature snowy owl had been seen at a power plant along the Ohio River. After staying there a few days, it had ventured to cross the expanse of water. Before dawn this morning, we'd heard it had been found floating in the river. A workman at the locks tied a rope to a life jacket and tossed it out to the presumably grateful owl. It had, amazingly, climbed aboard, allowed itself to be towed in, and taken flight. I wanted to see it before it did anything that stupid again.

Snowy owls that find themselves in such southern climes are often immature birds, inexperienced, exhausted, even starving. It is believed that many don't survive their wanderings. I'm glad I didn't know that when I was chasing snowies in my formative New England birding years. Such a delight, to see the huge pink house on the road to Plum Island, Massachusetts, crowned with a living finial, one with Eskimo eyes and a black-barred down parka, squinting against the late winter sun.

Liam screamed all the way to the owl, a forty-minute jaunt. Fritos and Tootsie Rolls bought me twenty minutes to drink in the owl's beauty as it perched on the gable of a boarded-up farmhouse. Very picturesque. It preened its disheveled

A Snowy Owl on the Pink House, Plum Island, Newburyport, MA

feathers, a good sign, I thought. I contemplated bringing it a roadkill or two. *Couldn't hurt, might help . . .* I managed a couple of sketches, in between resupplying snacks and cajoling Liam to stay in his car seat by the busy roadside.

Too soon, Liam reached escape velocity and volume, and we pushed toward home. The owl gave us a cold stare as we left. I decided to take the scenic route, a maze of washboard gravel roads and deep Appalachian "hollers." I nipped in to bird an embayment of the Ohio. Catching sight of the water, Liam paused. "Srowing."

"What, honey?"

"Srowing. Srowing. SROWING."

"Mommy, he wants to throw rocks in the water," Phoebe translated. A two-year-old boy's idea of a good time. I pulled over and freed him, gathered a great pile of gravel, and seated him by the bank of the embayment to toss rocks. Blessed silence, peace. I watched a couple of ring-billed gulls plunge-diving, a hooded merganser sneaking through the shadows of a cut bank. A killdeer keened, stopped, bobbed. Liam plunked. Phoebe floated log boats.

An hour passed. I tried not to think of the owl and my sketchbook. We belted up and headed for home. Liam screamed all the way up Newell's Run, all the way up Cow Run (the southern Ohio way of naming creeks and the roads that invariably run along them). Some cattle hove into view. The screaming stopped for a moment, and a soft *moo* sounded from the back seat. Frazzled as I was, I had to smile. We stopped to look at a tolerant bull just on the other side of a low electric fence.

We pushed on. Liam howled. I turned up the classical music and thought of a time in South Texas, when Liam was only seven months old and Phoebe was the one who stayed home with a sitter. On a nature walk at Santa Ana National Wildlife Reserve, Liam stuffed into a backpack, I struggled to keep up with the group. John Acorn, the "Nature Nut" of television fame, led us, pointing out birds and butterflies with humor and wildwood savvy. I adore him and was delighted to be along. But Liam was hungry, and I was blessed with the ability to supply just what he needed. Telling John to press on, I sat down on the concrete path with Liam. Peace and silence settled over the Texas swampland. I had twenty minutes to soak it all in.

My first
bobcat
April 2000
Sta. Ana NWR, Texas
Stepped out of the brush while I
was nursing Liam!

A soft crackling of leaves, a rustle of grasses. A large male bobcat, spotted and barred and flamed with orange on the insides of his legs, stepped out of the brush less than twenty feet away. He paused, soft paws on the concrete, and swiveled his lovely head. Slit eyes fell on us, mother and child. In the cool way of the wild, he registered nothing, did not flinch, continued sweeping the scene. He flicked his stumpy tail and padded across the path. Once in cover, he paused and looked back, eyes wide this time. We connected. My soul whooped silently, and I wanted to un-latch Liam, hold him up, show him his first, my first, beautiful bobcat, an animal I had waited all my life to see. But for Liam I'd never have stopped in silence to wait for him.

It's such a good metaphor for raising children, this bobcat encounter. Yes, ba-bies can be taxing. They take lots of time, sometimes all of it. They specialize in inconveniencing their parents. It's their job. But such rewards await the faithful. I know that soon enough Liam will reach the age of reason, when he can speak Eng-lish instead of screaming, when he'll be able to wait more than a heartbeat for gratification, when he, too, is peering through a scope at his first green jay, lifting my heart with his gasp of surprise. Fool that I am, I guess I'll keep taking the kids along.

The Healing Walk

I TOOK A WALK TODAY in the cold, sharp air, the first walk I've taken alone since last spring. Odd to think that living as we do on eighty acres of woodland and meadow, walks can be so hard to come by. The summer was hot, I was pregnant, the hills are steep. By May, the goldenrod and bluestem grass are tall enough to cross and cut against my thighs on the unmown path over the neighbor's land, and by June, it's more like a wade than a walk. Cantilever the weight out front, and a long walk with one's leaden belly for company is not an appealing prospect.

By November 8, the reason I was not walking had arrived. It was the perfect season to hunker down in the house with fluffy blankets and mugs of tea, midday movies, and endless feeding sessions. While our first child, Phoebe, could amuse herself for long stretches in a baby seat just watching me work, Liam takes being put down as just that: a put-down. His lower lip sticks out and trembles, and he lets me know that I was put on the earth to *hold* him all day long. *Oh, I had other plans for at least part of the time, dear baby.* Cabin fever crept in and curled itself around my ankles. Much as I love my apple-cheeked boy and red-haired girl, I had to get out of the house this morning.

Snow drifted gently down beneath a weak winter sun that struggled and failed to cut through the pearly clouds. Grainy snow collected in the curled leaves and

golden-
crowned
Kinglet—
fairy come to life

a little
farham,
surprised at
in the open
2/11/00

showed the tracery of fox and squirrel, junco and crow. An inane bit of music from one of Phoebe's television shows played itself over and over in my head, in rhythm to the tramp of my boots, until the three-part note of a golden-crowned kinglet mercifully changed the channel. The hiss of drifting snowflakes, kinglet music. Much better. My long-idle primitive brain flickered back to life, pushed aside the crowded, mostly pointless thoughts that clutter my head, and began to help me see.

He was feeding at the foot of a steep hill when I saw him, a small fork-horned buck with a neat white ring around his muzzle and a bib of white at his throat. I stopped, and his head came up. He looked around, failed to see me, and dropped his head again. Slowly I raised my binoculars and studied his smooth, high-rising antlers, his moist brown eyes, the whiskers on his chin. He became aware of my presence, though the wind was in my favor, and he dropped his head, then quickly jerked it back up, as if to fool me into moving. He took three steps toward me, looking nervously to the side. I saw the realization creep into his eyes, here at the tail end of hunting season, that he'd really blown it this time.

There is a scene in *The Outlaw Josey Wales*, a movie I've watched at least six times in the past month, in which Sondra Locke's character is cornered by a nasty band of Comancheros who are looking to take her prisoner and sell her to Ten Bears, a Comanche chief. She doesn't know that, of course; she just knows her worst nightmare has come, and her huge blue eyes get wider and more terrified by the second, though she doesn't move a muscle.

In this little buck's tapered face and great brown eyes, I saw that look, saw him searching for a way out where there was none. Never taking his eyes off me, he swung his hindquarters around behind him and leaned behind a tree trunk. Then he moved forward to put the brow of the hill between us should I be lining up my shot. Even as I realized what he was doing and marveled at his ability to protect his vulnerable chest and flanks, I felt abashed. *I should let him know I mean him no harm*, I thought. So I lowered my binoculars and spoke to him. "It's okay. I'm not a hunter." His ears twitched. I spoke again. He held his ground, growing more Sondra-like by the second. I held my hands up and wiggled my fingers. "You can go now." He sprang to the side as though shot from a cannon, white flag high, windy snorts tearing from his nose, broken branches flying in his wake. I felt as though I'd granted him something, though his life was not mine to grant. Perhaps our encounter would get him through what was left of this hunting season, and maybe that was thanks enough to him, for letting me take in his beauty.

A few yards farther on, and I am breathing to the tramp of my feet, reveling in the memory of the flying buck. A rustle in the leaves and a ruffed grouse explodes into flight, then glides like a crazy biplane down a hill before me. Its fanned tail is red-brown. In nine years of looking, I've never seen a gray phase grouse here. In Connecticut and Massachusetts, the grouse were mostly gray. It's likely linked to thermoregulation: Red radiates more heat than gray, and southern Ohio is a lot milder in winter than New England.

Whether it's true or not, I like the feel of the theory in my head; it's better than the thoughts that usually take up my mental real estate, like *Now where is the missing piece to that Ernie puzzle?*

More fox tracks, not in a very neat line, though, and a little staggery. Could he be carrying something? A grouse, perhaps? Squirrel tracks intersecting the fox tracks. A red-tailed hawk calls hoarsely, *Throwing a spear at me*, as my father would say. There was always a redtail at this place last winter, too. I reach the Chute, my name for a steep little glen where a perennial stream rollicks over stair-stepped sandstone. It's all iced over, but water flows beneath, making amazing fishlike swimming shapes beneath a thick glaze. I wish Phoebe were with me so we could watch them bloop by. It's a natural lava lamp, mesmerizing, made for the open gaze of a three-year-old.

I start up the steep hill toward our orchard and home and have to take off my gloves to dump some heat in the midteens chill. I'm out of shape, but I make it fine, happy not to be heavy anymore, happy to be going home to my apple-cheeked baby and red-haired girl. A forty-five-minute vacation, unrepeatable in any detail, precious and rare.

These are the sights I've missed seeing, thoughts I've missed having. It's good to be home.

Catching Paul

I WAS PICKING OVER the green beans when I saw it—a flutter of wings against the banks of fluorescent lights in the grocery store ceiling overhead. My heart sank, as it always does, to see a bird in a grocery store. I muttered a wish that it would be a house sparrow, but my bird watcher's eye had already decided it wasn't. I followed it through to the store's bakery counter, where I eventually located it, perched calmly in a revolving rack of birthday candles. I smiled when my eye fell upon it. In the little wire candle tree it had found the only remotely shrublike structure in the entire store and was quite well hidden amid the Barney and Blue's Clues birthday decorations. I could see just a part of its breast—white, heavily streaked with brown. Song sparrow, I decided, just as it took off over the beverage aisle, headed back to produce.

Now, a sparrow, even a song sparrow, can live a mighty long time in a grocery store. Years, I'd guess, if the management doesn't decide to do it in as a health hazard. It's got everything it needs, except, of course, freedom, a decent habitat, a mate, and other sparrows to hang out with. It can nibble the fresh kale and lettuce, peck the apples and grapes, scrounge for spilled seed in the pet and wild-bird sections. It can drink and even bathe in the automatic mist hissing down on the salad greens. It can hide in the candle rack or the houseplants, perch in the high

Paul, at the candle rack at
Kroger's bakery. October 2001

light fixtures at the slightest hint of threat. Make no mistake, it's probably pretty un-happy, but it survives. The chances of its finding its way out through the double front doors or the heavy swinging loading dock doors are about nil. This store backs up onto a marsh preserve, and I guessed the sparrow had entered via the darkened loading dock and flown toward the lighted store proper when the swinging doors opened. I wanted to get it out of there.

Quercus
coccinea
Scarlet oak

I began asking around in the bakery section, where the ladies were quite forthcoming. "He's been in here about a week," one told me. "He's just as tame as can be. He'll let you come up and talk to him as close as you are to me, but you'd better not have a bass net in your hand!" She motioned to a large aluminum-handled fishing net leaning against the pastry counter. "He knows when you're after him, and he doesn't want anything to do with you if you've got that net in your hand."

I could sense the respect in her voice, respect for a tiny brown bird. "I named him Paul," she added a little sheepishly. *Paul.* It was the perfect name for this modest sparrow, and it told me volumes about how she felt about him.

I came back the next day with a sparrow trap, one designed to rid the premises of house sparrows. Baited with seed or bread, it's a simple wire box with a spring-loaded lid. When the bird jumps down onto a treadle, the lid slams shut and the sparrow is yours. I set it, mounded seed enticingly inside, and put it atop a doughnut case next to the birthday candle rack. I left my number with the bakery

Rhus copallina
Winged sumac

Acer rubrum
Red maple

Sassafras albidum
Sassafras

Acer rubrum
Red maple

ladies and the store manager. A week later, I still hadn't gotten a call, so I returned. The trap was still open, unsprung. Paul had cleaned up all the stray seed around the outside but hadn't so much as stuck a toe inside the trap. This was going to be harder than I thought.

The store manager expressed his frustration. "Used to be when we'd get a bird in here I'd just turn out all the store lights in the morning before anybody got here and open the loading dock doors, and out it would go, heading for the light. I got rid of any number of birds that way. But since they remodeled, a computer controls all the lights and I can't override it. I can't even turn out the lights in my own store!" I pondered the implications of this statement. The situation seemed to me to be akin to a car whose windows couldn't be rolled down. This sounded like a plan that made sense at corporate headquarters, but not in the field. I assured the manager I'd try my best to catch the sparrow some other way.

I took the trap home and rigged up two red plastic jar lids. One I taped to the top of the trap and partially filled with seed. The other I taped just inside the trap chamber so it could be reached with a short hop down into the chamber. This would accustom Paul to entering the chamber, even if he only had to hop an inch inside it. Finally, I wired the trap open so it could not spring shut. I wanted the trap to become Paul's happy place, his kitchen. I left it there for five days.

When I came back to check the trap, Paul had been in the store for over a month. The bakery ladies were ready for me, their eyes shining. "I'm not so sure you'll ever catch him," one woman said. "He sits on the trap all day, but he doesn't go inside it."

"We'll see about that," I answered. I climbed up and retrieved the trap from the top of the doughnut case. Both food dishes were completely empty. Seed hulls were littered all around the cage. Paul had definitely been inside the trap chamber and he would go in again. And when he did, he'd be mine.

This time, I taped a jar lid directly to the treadle inside the trap chamber and filled it with millet, sunflower, cracked corn, and peanut butter suet dough. It was irresistible fare for a hungry sparrow. In the lid atop the trap I put a meager single serving of the same food. Cackling, I climbed back up and replaced Paul's kitchen.

"You know, that crazy bird will light on the trays of hot rolls just out of the big oven," a baker told me. "I'll try to shoo him off, but he comes right back. And he goes way back into the deli. I don't know what he's after, but he's not scared of anything and he knows his way around here pretty good." There was obvious affection in her voice. She lowered it conspiratorially. "I just feel sorry for him, though, and I'm afraid one of these guys is going to try to get him one day." I grasped her meaning immediately. It can't be within the health code to have a sparrow hopping around on the bakery trays.

I reassured her. "I predict that Paul will be in that trap by tomorrow morning." It was noon when I left the store.

I was finishing up the dinner dishes at 6:20 P.M. when the phone rang. It was the store's manager, and he was clearly excited. "Is this Julie, with the bird trap?" he asked.

"Yes, it is!" I answered.

"Well, we have a bird in the trap!"

I whooped with joy. "I told you! I told you I'd get him! That's fantastic! Hang on to him while I call my husband! He'll be by in a couple of minutes to pick him up."

I hung up and did a dance of joy around the kitchen. Phoebe and Liam danced, too, hollering and whooping. "WE GOT HIM! WE GOT HIM! WE GREEN AND YELLOW GOT HIM!" we sang.

We turned on the porch light and waited breathlessly for Bill. He came in, leading with the trap, a frantic Paul ricocheting around inside. I clutched the trap and peered inside. Paul gave a small peep of fear, and there was something familiar about his voice. His brow was faintly yellow, his streaking too fine, his belly too white . . . he was altogether too small . . . *This is no song sparrow*, I realized. "Hey! This is a Savannah sparrow!" I exclaimed, agog. What were the odds? An uncommon migrant through the Mid–Ohio Valley at best, a Savannah sparrow would be one of the last birds I'd expect to see perched atop a birthday candle rack or a tray of hot buns.

"I'll be darned," Bill said. "I didn't get a chance to look at him in the excitement, but he didn't look much like a song sparrow to me when I picked him up."

Carefully, I reached into the trap and brought Paul out into the light. So tiny, so sleek, so . . . *fat*. His high-carb diet had clearly agreed with him. Paul was padded. I took a bad snapshot of him clutched in one hand, then released him to the comparative comfort of a pet carrier, its floor covered with straw and natural perches. He settled down quickly and enjoyed his first dark night in more than a

month. His temporary home had been a twenty-four-hour establishment; the lights never went out. I imagined all Paul had been through and what he must have been thinking. Was he thankful for the darkness? Glad for the feel of straw and wood beneath his feet? Happy for the quiet, away from humming refrigerator cases and floor buffers and the incessant beep of scanners? Aware that he was one heck of a lucky bird? Wondering what would become of him in the morning?

At 8:00 A.M., we donned coats and shoes and solemnly trooped out the front door with Paul's carrier. Liam said, "I want to see that bird fly!" Phoebe made sure she would be the one to open the carrier door. Paul hesitated, then shot out like a streaky brown arrow to the top of a birch tree, its leaves golden and drooping in a warm November drizzle. He looked down, up, all around. A few goldfinches settled in beside him. For twenty minutes Paul perched, his feet fumbling on the twigs, feet that were now more used to the feel of plastic and metal. He watched the juncos and goldfinches, the song sparrows and cardinals. He watched me scattering millet beneath his tree, talking softly to him. Then Paul wiped his bill, gave a soft *tweet*, and was gone, flying straight and true out over the meadow, headed south.

Index